B2B eCommerce MasterPlan

How to make wholesale eCommerce a key part of your business to business sales growth

CHLOË THOMAS

Kernu Publishing

© Chloë Thomas
Originally published 2017
Kernu Publishing
PO Box 740
Truro
Cornwall
TR1 9HE
United Kingdom

All rights reserved. Apart from limited use for private study, teaching, research, criticism or review, no part of this publication may be reproduced, stored or transmitted without the prior permission in writing of the copyright owner and publisher of this book.

ISBN: 978-1-9998788-0-1

Reviews of B2B eCommerce MasterPlan:

"Embarking on your eCommerce journey as any type of business can be incredibly daunting. But B2B eCommerce MasterPlan clearly and thoroughly lays out everything you need to know to get started adding this important new revenue stream to your business. With everything from how to create your online product inventory to how to deal with falling out with your web developers, this book will hold your hand every step of the way!"
Neil Cocker - CEO, ramptshirts.com

"If you're selling goods B2B and you're not doing it online, you should be and Chloe's most recent book explains why. This book contains all the information you need to make informed decisions and be confident you're heading in the right direction. Chloe explains the pros of B2B e-commerce in a clear, easy-to-digest and encouraging way. Even if you've been in B2B e-commerce for a while, you'll find something in here to take away and apply to your site. Well worth a read."
Steve Nixon, Dayex, Ecommerce Manager, dayex.co.uk

"B2B is such an important part of any business and just relying on field reps to grow your business is no longer an option in 2017. As we all know websites are now not just a part of any business but one of the most important parts especially when it comes to business growth. Providing a first class B2B website is no different and a necessity if your company wants to stay ahead of the competition in the future. I was therefore so excited when Chloe announced that she was building on her already successful B2C book series and delving into the relatively unknown world of B2B eCommerce with her latest book.

Those that are in B2B businesses know that B2B eCommerce truly is different than B2C eCommerce. In B2B, we have complex customers, complex products, and we have complex systems. This book does a fantastic job of detailing the reasons and tactics behind building and operating a B2B eCommerce site. I was incredibly impressed by the depth and case studies"

Justin King, founder, eCommerceandB2B.com, Senior Partner at B2X Partners

"The book is structured in such a way it becomes the blueprint to building a B2B website the correct way and walks you through all the successes and pitfalls you will face on your journey. It will definitely save you time, money, loads of stress and hopefully cut down on those sleepless night you will experience. Chloe is an excellent author and eCommerce Guru and this book is testimony to her ongoing success."

Rob Boyle, Digital Marketing Manager, Qualtex UK Ltd (Replacement Parts and Spares for Domestic Appliances) www.qualtexuk.com

"As a 10 year veteran of B2B ecommerce with multiple online stores, this book made me chuckle with the honesty and the real-life advice. Nothing could prepare you for this journey into the unknown. That was until Chloe wrote this step-by-step guide. Back in my day, you had to just figure it out by trial and error with the added costs of time and failure.

In fact, some of (what I thought were) my own personal trade secrets are now listed in the book for everyone to know. It took me years to figure those out. Please don't let my competitors read it.

This book is a godsend as it covers all ends of the process without any fluff. You could create your entire project management process from the book. If you don't have a successful B2B online presence, you MUST have Chloe's book."

Jon Butt - Managing Director - FireProtectionOnline.co.uk

"As someone who has had a B2B ecommerce website for many years is and is now on version four I know how full of expensive pitfalls the process can be. Chloe has written is an invaluable guide to these pitfalls and how to avoid them. Do not even begin the process without reading this book. Chloe takes you through all the stages from deciding exactly what you need, to choosing the right partner to launching your new website. An excellent guide."

Kate Turner, Founder, Partypacks.co.uk

Forword

Back in 1999 when I launched my business, the concept of *being a specialist provider of B2B eCommerce solutions* raised a few eyebrows. After all, surely B2B eCommerce provision wasn't really that different from B2C?

Nearly two decades later, the true complexity – and potential rewards – of an integrated B2B solution are much more widely appreciated. Indeed, far from being a niche, specialist provider, we now find ourselves at the forefront of the biggest growth area in eCommerce.

Over the years, we've helped customers and prospects understand the differences and similarities between B2B and B2C eCommerce. We've helped companies clarify their objectives and advised on the best ways to realise the benefits that come with adopting best practice. And we've helped businesses of all kinds through the successful transition to eCommerce.

Today, as buying habits continue to change, B2B eCommerce is shifting from a nice-to-have, to a must-have and has become a boardroom priority for many manufacturers, wholesalers and distributors. Yet despite its rise up the corporate agenda, the complexities of B2B eCommerce still raise a raft of familiar questions.

With the release of **B2B eCommerce MasterPlan**, there is now a single authoritative text that addresses the challenges businesses need to overcome when they embark on a B2B eCommerce initiative. This book provides practical advice on how to approach each stage of planning and implementation, and also offers valuable guidance on ensuring that activities remain optimised after launch. It will be required reading for everyone at Aspidistra and copies will go to all our existing clients as well as prospects.

I particularly enjoyed *Chapter 10, Lessons in Site Building* – it certainly mirrors our own experience. As Chloe explains, some polite friction between the business and the website builder is inevitable but following this book's guidance on preparation, specification and communication, should help to keep it to a minimum.

I'm also reminded of a story I heard about a website redesign, where a graphic designer who had never designed for eCommerce undertook the work. While the new site looked attractive enough, unfortunately it broke many of the paradigms of eCommerce. For example, the previously obvious 'Buy' button was replaced by a dull grey graphic, and the 'Login' button was moved and changed to another obscure graphic. Such changes confused existing buyers and discouraged new customers.

If this book had been in print at the time, I could have sent the company a copy. Chloe's *Top Tips for making it easier to buy on your website* would have ensured the design focus was on sales support, not sales prevention!

Paul Dorey, MD, Aspidistra Software Ltd

aspidistra
S O F T W A R E

Aspidistra creates B2B eCommerce solutions for organisations of all sizes. Their platforms integrate with Sage 50 and 200, ERP 1000 and Pegasus Opera, while solutions for SAP B1 Navision and Sage Live are also scheduled for launch in the near future. The company is recognised as an industry innovator and regularly brings new integrations to market.

Whatever your reasons for reading this book, if you're looking to get in touch with a specialist provider that can help you navigate the challenges and opportunities of B2B eCommerce, give Aspidistra a call on +44 1548 856583.

sales@aspidistra.com

www.aspidistra.com

Contents

Introduction   19
Who have I written this book to help? Why am I Qualified to write this book? Not sure B2B eCommerce is for you? You know B2B eCommerce is for you. Already got a B2B eCommerce site live? What's in the book? Getting the most from the book

STAGE ONE: Should You Add Ecommerce to Your Business?   31

Chapter 1: What Is B2B? Why Should You Care?   33
What is B2B? Why is it an important distinction? What is eCommerce? What is B2B eCommerce then? Is it all that different from 'normal' B2C eCommerce? Why should you care about how eCommerce can increase your profits? B2B buyers (your customers) are increasingly buying and researching online. The B2B eCommerce market is growing fast. You can get in ahead of your competition. And get new customers.

Chapter 2: The 4 Reasons to Adopt B2B eCommerce   43
Reason 1: The new breed of B2B buyers; Reason 2: Competitive Pressure and Industry Shift; Reason 3: Your Customers want it; Reason 4: Pressure from within the business; Why should you add a B2B eCommerce operation to your business and work to make it a success?

Chapter 3: Case Study: Upgrade Bikes "What's going to help our B2B customer sell more?"   55

STAGE TWO: Getting Everyone And Everything Ready   61

Chapter 4: The Objectives: Who's the Customer?   65

Chapter 5: Team Impact: Getting them Ready   71
The Sales Team; The call centre team; The Marketing Team; The IT Team; New Roles; How to facilitate these conversations; Do you need to hire the skills and knowledge in?

Chapter 6: What You Need to Have Ready Before Your Site Can Be a Reality   77
Pricing; Delivery; Stock information; Product Information; Transferring data from a catalogue; Transferring data from a B2C eCommerce site; Manufacturers Information; General product information tips; Product Images; Getting the photos ready for the website; Specialist Product Information; Product Structure; Customer Database or CRM (Customer Relationship Management System); Marketing Plans and Budgets.

Chapter 7: B2B eCommerce Site Structure Options   95
Open eCommerce Site; Shop Window with Trade Accounts Login; Open eCommerce Site with Trade Accounts Login; Closed Trade-Only Portal; Website Spin Offs; A White Label / Distributor Option; Full product feed; Hybrids / Custom Builds for Customers

Chapter 8: Case Study: Industrial Ancillaries "People still buy from people"   113

STAGE THREE: Making the Website a Reality   119

Chapter 9: What Does the Website Need to Do?   121
Direct order from product category; Easy order lists; Upload order by spreadsheet; Quick order SKU look-up; Repeat past orders; Personal best seller list; Current offers section.

Chapter 10: Lessons in Site Building   129
You will fall out; When the site finally goes live, you'll want to hug your site builders; The last week before the site goes live will be crazy; Timescales will stretch; Something not in the brief will turn out to be critical; However good your brief is, it will change; Your site will never be finished; Must be a great site on day one.

Chapter 11: 7 Steps to get Your Site Built Right First Time   135
Step 1: Research: Consult the stakeholders; Step 2: Creating the brief; Step 3: Deciding who to send the tender to: Create your Long List, Create your Short List; Step 4: Running the Tender Process: Sending out the tender, Whilst waiting on responses, Picking who gets to meet with you, Emailing the unsuccessful, Emailing the successful & setting up the meetings, Meetings week, The Final Decision, Email the unsuccessful; Step 5: Signing and kicking off; Step 6: The build; Step 7: Putting the new site live.

Chapter 12: Case Study: Gloveman VIP "It's a tool, not a be-all, end-all replacement"   169

STAGE FOUR: Making B2B eCommerce a Success: Site launch and Ongoing Marketing 177

Chapter 13: Launch Is not Live 179
What is launch? Launch is only the beginning

Chapter 14: Lessons in Marketing 183
B2B and B2C eCommerce Marketing are the same; Segmentation; What sort of customer are they? What the person's role is in the buyer organisation? Chloë's Promotional Golden Rule; Other promotional tips; Clear Calls to Action; Social proof; Scarcity; Deadlines; Free delivery; Sales or Marketing? The site is a new order-taking channel, being online opens up lots of new ways to drive sales; Onboarding will be key; Retention is critical; Social Media: How personal should it be? Marketing to the end customer

Chapter 15: 6 Steps to Plan & Execute Your Launch   199
Step 1: Objectives – what do you want your launch to achieve?: Who, What, The numbers, More than one objective; Step 2: Budget – How much can you afford to spend? Step 3: Message – What do you want to say to your customers? Step 4: Marketing Methods - How will you get the message out there? Likely channels for getting the message to existing customers, Likely channels for getting the message to new customers; Step 5: Plan – What are you going to do? A calendar of promotional activity, A written guide to the plan, The target tracking dashboard; Step 6: Execute – Time to make the plan work; What happens after launch?

Chapter 16: Case Study: Ramp Tshirts
"Less than 20% of our sales come from people who have zero human interaction pre-purchase"   221

Chapter 17: BONUS: What Successful Websites Need...   227

The role of your website; How do you increase your conversion rate? Make it easier for customers to buy; Top tips for making it easier to buy on your website; Trust; CRO: The ongoing process of making it easier to buy on your website: 1 Find a barrier, 2 Identify a fix, 3 Apply the fix, 4 Does it work? A few extra CRO tips

Chapter 18: BONUS: Should You Launch a B2C eCommerce Site?   241

Website differences; Different product information needs; Different pricing needs; Different checkouts; Payment methods; Warehouse and customer services differences; The marketing differences; The financial differences; The big one: What about your B2B customers? Is there a B2C eCommerce option for you?

List of Case Studies   249

Glossary   251

About the Author   253

Other Books by Chloë Thomas   257

The eCommerce MasterPlan Podcast   259

Author's Thanks

I have to start with Paul Dorey, Sue Haswell and the team at Aspidistra – if they hadn't given me the push to write this book, and sewn the idea in my head it wouldn't have happened, and I'm really pleased with how it's turned out.

Thank you to my awesome book creation team for helping me get another book out there to help my readers. Liz – you always get the cover brief spot on, Doug – you are 100% my go to for all things copy, paperback and ebook!, Joni – you do just as good a job with the illustrations as Liz does with the cover. And, last but not least, Kyran, Izabela & the Music Radio Creative Team for making me sound so great in the audiobook. Between you, you make the book production process a dream.

(If anyone reading wants intros – let me know)

And a big thank you to my partner Jonno for putting up with my eCommerce obsession, and going to a friends to watch the grand prix when I had to spend that Sunday proofing this book!

Finally, thank you to all the B2B eCommerce people I've worked with and discussed with over the years, especially my podcast guests and research interviewees for this book.

Introduction

BEFORE YOU DIVE into the content, take a read of this section to help you make the most of this book.

eCommerce and online marketing are constantly changing, so I've designed the book to help you take the right approach no matter what changes.

Who Have I Written This Book to Help?

B2B businesses looking to harness eCommerce to grow their profit.

As I've been researching, preparing, and writing this book, I've had three types of business in mind:

1. The B2B companies that are currently selling everything offline. Using catalogues, price lists, a call centre, and with reps out on the road drumming up those sales. Every order is placed by a customer contacting

one of your team (by phone, email, fax, etc.) who puts the order into the system for them.

2. The B2B companies that are already on the journey to having an eCommerce arm. Maybe you've taken the site live and it's going well, but you know there is more to come; maybe you're the only one in the business who sees the light and you're busy trying to convince the others to agree to it!

3. The B2C eCommerce Wholesaler – the business that, as well as selling to consumers via their own website (and/or physical store), is also selling the product in bulk to other retailers[1].

The book is written for the first two, but is still well worth a read if you're in the third group.

This third group is particularly interesting: 10 years ago, if you'd created a cool new product, you'd have started shifting units by selling to existing retailers or distributors. These days, the creators of those cool new products are starting off by both selling direct to consumers online AND shifting units through wholesaling to other retailers and outlets.[2]

If you believe enabling your business customers to place orders and buy from you online is part of your organisation's future – read on!

---

[1] In this case, I'm excluding marketplaces, so Amazon FBA doesn't count. This is where you're selling to a number of health food stores, or gyms, etc.

[2] We've had a few such businesses on the podcast – have a listen to how Miso Tasty, TeaShed, Naturalicious and more have done this at eCommerceMasterPlan.com/podcast

Why Am I Qualified to Write This Book?

For over a decade I've been working in the field of eCommerce strategy and marketing. Owning and running companies that sold products and services to other businesses. The clients and customers I've worked for are a mixture of B2B and B2C, most of which have been in the eCommerce space.

I've helped a number of businesses through the decision of whether or not to adopt an eCommerce channel into their business. Brick and mortar retailers looking to reach a greater geographic spread of customers without having to open more physical stores. Wholesalers, distributors and product manufacturers who want to make an informed decision about whether eCommerce is the right next move for them, and then how to implement it to maximise the success of the operation.

Now my time is spent at eCommerce MasterPlan where I aim to help eCommerce business owners, managers and marketers to make the right decisions for their business. I've written a number of books about eCommerce as a whole, which are mainly focused on the B2C business. Those have been read by many a B2B marketer who has asked me for something more specific to their sector. And this is it.

In getting ready to write this book I've looked back over the projects I've worked on in B2B eCommerce, and the experiences I've had as a B2B marketer. I've reviewed the podcast interviews I've done with B2B eCommerce businesses, and they form many of the examples and references in the book (giving you the opportunity to dive a little deeper into their stories) and one of the case studies.

That gave me a lot of what I needed to write the book – but I also knew I wanted to speak to those actively running large B2B eCommerce operations about how they've found the transition and both the good and the bad they experienced along the way. Plus I've chatted to a number of B2B specialist website builders to get their perspective too. The on and off the record elements of those conversations have been really useful to put this book together – and three of the on-the-record conversations are detailed in the three case studies you'll find in the book.

Finally, in the final stages of putting this book together I've had a number of hands on B2B marketers review it and give me their feedback.

All that research and testing I hope has ensured this book will meet your needs, and help you grow your business with the aid of eCommerce.

Not yet decided whether B2B eCommerce is for you?

This book will enable you to work out whether it's for you or not. It will:

- Outline the potential benefits.
- Outline what you need to do to make it successful.

Lots of case studies of those who've already been through the process (including what went wrong!).

I suggest you read the whole thing to help you make up your mind.

Then, if you decide it is for you, use the book as your handbook as you work through each stage.

You know B2B eCommerce is for you

You're a YES, but you have not yet started on the journey. The book will:

- Outline the steps you need to take.

- Show how to make sure the business is fully ready to embrace this new way to service your customers.

- Answer the question: Just what sort of website do you need?

- Itemize how to make it all happen.

- Illustrate how to go live.

- Detail the launch process – and the marketing that will make it a success.

I suggest you read the whole thing before you start to implement anything.

Then use the book as your handbook as you work through each stage.

Already Got a B2B eCommerce Site Live?

Your B2B eCommerce website is live – and you want more! The book will let you:

- Check what you've already done against the content here – what could you do better?
- Follow the marketing ideas to grow the online sales, and decrease the offline costs.
- Consider whether it's time to start selling to consumers too?

I would still recommend reading through the whole book (at some point) as you'll almost certainly find ideas in each section that will help you.

But it is written in a way that allows you to just jump into each of the chapters as you need them.

Start with the areas you feel you're weakest in, then identify the ideas that will help the most and get it actioned.

What's in the Book?

It's going to be your all-round bible to B2B eCommerce that sits on your desk and you come back to again and again.

It will take you through the 4 Stages you and your business need to go through to successfully add a B2B eCommerce operation that complements and supports your whole business so that sales, and profits, and customer satisfaction all increase.

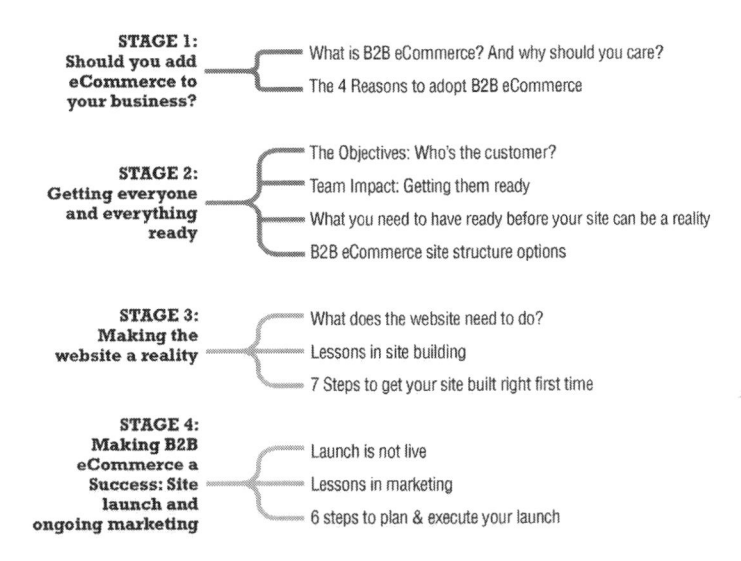

STAGE 1: Should you add eCommerce to your business?
- What is B2B eCommerce? And why should you care?
- The 4 Reasons to adopt B2B eCommerce

STAGE 2: Getting everyone and everything ready
- The Objectives: Who's the customer?
- Team Impact: Getting them ready
- What you need to have ready before your site can be a reality
- B2B eCommerce site structure options

STAGE 3: Making the website a reality
- What does the website need to do?
- Lessons in site building
- 7 Steps to get your site built right first time

STAGE 4: Making B2B eCommerce a Success: Site launch and ongoing marketing
- Launch is not live
- Lessons in marketing
- 6 steps to plan & execute your launch

Stage 1: Should you add eCommerce to your business?

In this stage I explain the key terms and what they mean (B2B and eCommerce). Then help you to work out if eCommerce should be added to your business.

Adding eCommerce as a sales channel is not an easy process you can't just put up a website and then go back to business as usual.

It's a lot of work that will change the day-to-day activities and mindset across the business. That means you have to be 100% sure the time to do this is now before you start.

We'll look at the main reasons why you should consider adding eCommerce to your B2B offerings.

Stage 2: Getting everything and everyone ready

Assuming by the end of Stage 1 you're confident that now is the time, this is the Stage that will take you through how to get the business ready to take that step.

Please don't dive straight into briefing a website – there's a lot you need to consider and get ready before your business is ready for that and here we'll go through each area you need to work on.

Stage 3: Making the Website a Reality

Now you are ready to expand into the eCommerce business model; it's time to get that website live, to make the whole idea a reality.

eCommerce is about selling products online and your website is core to that, so there's lots that it must achieve to make the whole thing a success.

Including displaying your products, getting the visitors to add those products to their basket, and also making sure they DO place the order.

This Stage will take you through the steps to take to get the right website for you – from pulling together the brief, to selecting the right website builder, and managing the whole project to the point the website is live.

Stage 4: Making it a success – the site launch and ongoing marketing

It is one thing to have a great B2B eCommerce site. It's quite another to make your customers visit it and get them to use it to place orders. That relies on how you launch and market the website.

This Stage will explain how to plan and run a great site launch (the initial marketing campaign to get your customers using the website), and also the marketing that follows afterwards.

Just like you can't just put a site live and hope customers will use it, you can't just run a launch then assume they'll keep on using it!

Bonus Chapters

There are two topics I just couldn't write this book without covering for you, so I've added them as bonus chapters (some of my pre-publication reviewers felt these were some of the most useful sections of the book!):

Making your website a success

In Stage 4 we covered how to get customers to use your website, and that doesn't end with the launch campaign.

You also need to keep working on the website to make sure it's doing as good a job as possible at serving your customers – helping them manage their account and keep buying!

This chapter will introduce you to the key systems and methods you should adopt to keep your site meeting your customers' expectations, and driving sales.

B2C eCommerce

If you've decided to add an eCommerce option for your B2B Customers, you may be thinking: 'Well, we might as well open it up to consumers too'.

That's another big decision, because it's another totally different business model, and usually requires two websites because the needs of the two consumers are so different.

In this bonus chapter I run through what you should think about before making the decision.

Getting the most from the book

Once you have worked through the areas that are key for you, then the whole book is structured so you can easily dip into the right part when you need it.

Throughout the book, where I have more information available outside the book itself that can help you, I've flagged it.

I have created workbooks to help you make the most of each section. Plus, I've included several useful templates and other resources for you to download and use. Please do make the most of these!

It is all available at eCommerceMasterPlan.com/freeb2b. Go there right now to get access to it all, and download the workbook before you start.

The eCommerce MasterPlan Podcast is PACKED with content and ideas that will help you; when there's a specific episode that will help, I've flagged it in the book. You can find all our podcast episodes at: eCommerceMasterPlan.com/Podcast

Enjoy!

STAGE ONE

Should You Add Ecommerce to Your Business?

ADDING ECOMMERCE FOR your B2B Customer does not just mean putting up a site and then going back to business as usual.

It's a lot of work and will change the day-to-day activities and mindset across the business. So, you need to be sure it's the right thing for you AND that now is the right time, before you start.

That's what this stage is about.

1 What Is B2B eCommerce? And Why Should You Care?

B2B.

eCommerce.

Two concepts that regularly cause confusion.

If I had a £1 for every time I'm asked what B2B means.... AND for every time someone thinks having a website with affiliate links to Amazon is eCommerce....

Given the confusion around the words, why on earth have I decided to write a book about it?

Well – because there are a lot of B2B eCommerce marketers (and wannabe B2B eCommerce marketers who contact me asking for help, expressing their frustration about the lack of content available for them to help them build their B2B eCommerce operation.

Let's clear up those definitions before we get any deeper into that.

What Is B2B?

B2B stands for Business to Business. It is used to refer to businesses that are selling to other businesses. E.g:

- Accountants
- Shop-fitters
- Builders merchants
- Product designers
- Manufacturers
- Wholesalers

As opposed to B2C (business to consumer), which are businesses selling to consumers. E.g:

- Supermarkets
- Shoe shops
- Restaurants
- Newspapers

These terms are not unique to retail and eCommerce.

Usually a business will be either B2B or B2C, because to do both often adds a lot of complexity because they are two different business models. It's an important distinction, because the way you market to, and serve a business as a customer is very different from how you market to and serve a consumer as a customer – even though they are often the same person.

Why Is It an Important Distinction?

Even when it's the same product or service that's being sold to B2B and B2C buyers, the process is very different. How a big company with multiple offices buys stationery is very different from how a student buys stationery:

- The number of people involved in the buying decision – one vs several.
- The payment method used – credit card vs invoice with purchase order.
- The volume of product bought – one pen vs a whole box.

Somewhere in the middle, you have businesses — like me — that buy like consumers buy. I buy stationery for my business from Amazon, Bureau Direct, and the high street.

What Is eCommerce?

eCommerce is:

- **A business:** Because you must take it seriously; you cannot just put a website live and assume you'll make millions. Success in eCommerce requires everything it takes to be successful in business – strategy, marketing, sales, ops, finance, IT etc., etc,

- **Selling products or services:** This includes physical products that get delivered through the post, or virtual products that get delivered online (think games, movies, software), services like ticket sales or dentist appointments, and of course SaaS (Software as a Service) – all those app and tool subscriptions to online services like MeetEdgar, Shopify, and Zoom.

- **Taking the order online:** This is the critical bit, the bit that is different. eCommerce is where the order is placed online. In B2C eCommerce, that means the payment happens online too. In B2B eCommerce, that's usually the ideal – but it might also be that the order is placed and the price added to the monthly invoice.

What Is B2B eCommerce Then?

It's when a business that sells products or services to other businesses uses an online system to take customer's orders.

Is it all that different from 'normal' B2C eCommerce?

B2B eCommerce has many similarities to B2C eCommerce:

- You use a website.
- You're selling to human beings.
- You must use marketing or sales to get the customer to the website.
- There must be product information on the website.

But there are some fundamental differences too, and how pronounced these are depends on how your B2B customers behave.

If you're selling curtain poles to interior designers like Walcot House, or selling jewellery-making equipment to jewellery designers like Beads Direct does, your B2B customers behave almost exactly like B2C consumers.

But if you are selling hygienic disposable gloves to chains of care homes like Gloveman does, or cycling equipment to Halfords like Urban Bike does, your B2B customers behave very differently and have very different needs than a B2C consumer.

For example, you need the website to be able to handle the different pricing options you give to your customers, so that's a bit more complex than B2C eCommerce. The standard B2C platforms may not be able to cope with the complexity you need.

That's why I wanted to write this book — to provide a source of advice tailored to the B2B eCommerce sector, rather than just generic eCommerce advice.

However your customers behave when they buy, launching a B2B eCommerce operation is launching a whole new business — you must make sure the team (at all levels) is trained and bought in, and you need to re-educate the customers.

It's a lot of work, and not a decision to be taken lightly. But done well, it can bring huge rewards: Saving time and salaries, increasing customer loyalty and satisfaction, increasing sales, reducing costs, and increasing those profits.

Depending on how you do it, going eCommerce can also open up your business to new customer groups. Those that are too small for it to be worthwhile to visit with a rep to take the order can now self-serve and order online. Several bigger companies are now making an online ordering system a requirement for their suppliers, too.

Why Should You Care About How eCommerce Can Increase Your Profits?

For the businesses I interviewed when researching this book, the benefits of, and reasons for, going eCommerce were primarily about improving the bottom line – increasing profits by:

- Increasing sales

- Getting new customers.

- Providing a better service to existing customers, leading to increased spend.

- Streamlining workflows within your business so the team spends less time on admin, and more time on income-generating activity.

- Making it as easy as possible for the customer to order as and when they chose.

- Attracting new customers by enabling them to see what you do.

The obvious operational customer services win is that, if you've got customers self-servicing themselves online, then they're not taking up the time of your team. So, your team can be redeployed to work harder on the bigger accounts, or go out and find you new customers.

But it's about a lot more than sales, profits and cost savings. It's really about giving your customers what they want in order to grow your business by both retaining existing customers, and finding new ones.

B2B eCommerce (and maybe B2C too) **will** form a part of the future of your business, sustained growth and profitability, and the research backs this up.

B2B buyers (your customers) are increasingly buying and researching online:

- 30% make half or more of their work purchases online today[3].

- 56% expect to make half or more of their purchases online in 3 years' time[4].

- 74% research half (or more) of their work purchases online before buying[5].

The B2B eCommerce market is growing fast:

- Forrester estimates that B2B eCommerce will top $1.1T and account for 12.1% of all B2B sales by 2020[6].

- It's already twice the size of B2C eCommerce, driven by manufacturers and wholesalers.

---

3   Q2 2014 Forrester / Internet Retailer B2B Buy-Side Survey. www.forbes.com/sites/louiscolumbus/2016/09/12/predicting-the-future-of-b2b-e-commerce/
4   Q2 2014 Forrester / Internet Retailer B2B Buy-Side Survey www.forbes.com/sites/louiscolumbus/2016/09/12/predicting-the-future-of-b2b-e-commerce/
5   Latest Trends in B2B E-Commerce Strategies and Tech Investment, Andy Hoar & Peter Sheldon, June 2015 (Forrester) www.ircecontent.com/assets/161/resources/Hoar_Sheldon1.pdf
6   Predicting The Future Of B2B E-Commerce, Louis Columbus, Sept 2016 www.forbes.com/sites/louiscolumbus/2016/09/12/predicting-the-future-of-b2b-e-commerce/

- 46% of manufacturers say eCommerce will be their primary sales channel by 2020[7].

You can get in ahead of your competition:

- 85% of B2B companies admit they are not yet fully utilizing eCommerce, even though they recognize that digital commerce is an important revenue opportunity[8].

And get new customers:

- In 2014, Forrester Consulting surveyed 100 U.S. firms that had implemented B2B over the previous 7 years, finding that 31% of the revenue from the eCommerce sites was believed to be incremental.

The time to do it is now.

---

7   Four51 Unveils "Manufacturing Commerce & Technology 2020" Research, March 2016 public.four51.com/four51-unveils-manufacturing-commerce-technology-2020-research/
8   The State of B2B E-Commerce: Stats Roundup, Chris Mitchell, July 2016 (Business to Community) http://b2c.news/xsNFAs

2 The 4 Reasons to Adopt B2B eCommerce

THERE ARE LOTS of reasons why you should add eCommerce to your B2B business. In this Stage, I'm going to take you through the main reasons.

For each, consider how it applies to your business. Is it relevant? Should you get involved in eCommerce to better serve your customers?

Reason 1: The New Breed of B2B Buyers

Some things will never change about B2B buyers. There's still going to be multiple people involved in many sales, budgets will still be tight, and there will still be purchase orders and invoice chasing. (sorry!)

For some clients and orders, it's still going to be very much worth your while to cover those motorway miles and spend the time getting to properly understand their needs.

However, online is playing an increasing part in every B2B transaction (whether it's completed online or offline).

B2B buyers are humans too

Every one of your B2B buyers also buys things as a consumer; they don't only exist in work hours – they are a normal human too!

- 80% of companies implementing B2B eCommerce believe that their customer expectations have changed due to B2C practices [9].

Your customers are using Amazon, John Lewis, eBay, Alibaba, Walmart – they're just normal people. And now that they've experienced the convenience of buying online, they want to use that in their business life too.

- 30% make half or more of their work purchases online today[10].

- 56% expect to make half or more of their purchases online in 3 years' time[11].

---

9   2013 B2B Commerce Survey – Insight Into Key Trends Include Customer Experience, Mobile and Online Growth, Jeri Kelley, April 2013 (Oracle). blogs.oracle.com/cx/2013-b2b-commerce-survey-insight-into-key-trends-include-customer-experience%2c-mobile-and-online-growth-v2

10 Q2 2014 Forrester / Internet Retailer B2B Buy-Side Survey. www.forbes.com/sites/louiscolumbus/2016/09/12/predicting-the-future-of-b2b-e-commerce/

11 Q2 2014 Forrester / Internet Retailer B2B Buy-Side Survey

This is great because it's going to make migrating customers to online ordering a bit easier. But it also means you can't just slap a site up and hope it works, you've got to offer as a good a service as they're used to online from day one, adapted to B2B buying needs. You can't neglect making the website work well.

B2B buyers like to research online & self-serve

The majority of B2B buyers are now researching their work purchases online before buying[12], regardless of how they are eventually going to make the purchase.

And they're spending more time researching on their own before they make contact. If the information they want to know about you/your products is not easily available, they will take their research and business elsewhere.

The good news is that 83% of them would prefer to research their purchases on your website, rather than via Google, blogs, social media, or anywhere else[13]. So, if you can provide a website that includes the details of all your products, it becomes a way to lock in their loyalty and get their business – both on and offline.

---

[12] Latest Trends in B2B E-Commerce Strategies and Tech Investment, Andy Hoar & Peter Sheldon, June 2015 (Forrester) www.ircecontent.com/assets/161/resources/Hoar_Sheldon1.pdf

[13] B2B E-Commerce Statistics & Latest Trends 2017, Feb 2017 (Avatar) www.avatarsyndicate.com/inline/b2b-e-commerce-statistics-latest-trends-2017/

Your customers are looking to you to make their working day simpler, and to make buying more convenient.

Reason 2: Competitive Pressure and Industry Shift

It's not just the customers who are pushing you to change your business model. In most industries, there is a shift already under way, especially acute if your competitors already offer online ordering.

Industry growth

The B2B eCommerce market is growing at a pace. *The Wall Street Journal* recently reported on how the growth is accelerating (in the USA). Over the 25 years leading up to 2015, eCommerce reached 9% of total B2B sales, and by 2020 (just 5 years) it's predicted to go to 12%. That might not sound like much, but it's a 33% increase in just 5 years[14].

That growth is fuelled by more customers choosing to buy online, from more B2B businesses launching their eCommerce operations, and from the growth of B2C eCommerce that is changing human behaviour.

There is a huge opportunity for the B2B business that gets online in the near future and catches this wave.

---

14 B2B E-Commerce Trends in 2017, Jan 2017 (WJS, Wall Street Journal) partners.wsj.com/ups/b2b-e-commerce-trends-in-2016/

The competitors you watch

What are they up to? If they've launched a B2B eCommerce site, they're going to be accelerating the behaviour change in your target market from offline person-to-person orders to online ordering. You've got to get there before your customers start shifting to the companies that give them the transaction method they want.

Has no one gone eCommerce yet in your niche? Then there's your opportunity to get ahead of the pack and differentiate.

The competitors you (probably) don't watch

I'm talking about those sites you don't think of as a competitor, but sell the same products, or products that serve the same purpose as the ones you sell.

Sites like Amazon, Alibaba, eBay – and many, many more. Go and take a look; are they selling your products? Or similar products that satisfy the same customer need?

If your customers/target customers are after quick, low-hassle ordering, why wouldn't they go there? If it's easier than buying from you?

Plus, they're actively making it easier for businesses to transact with them – take a look at Amazon Business.

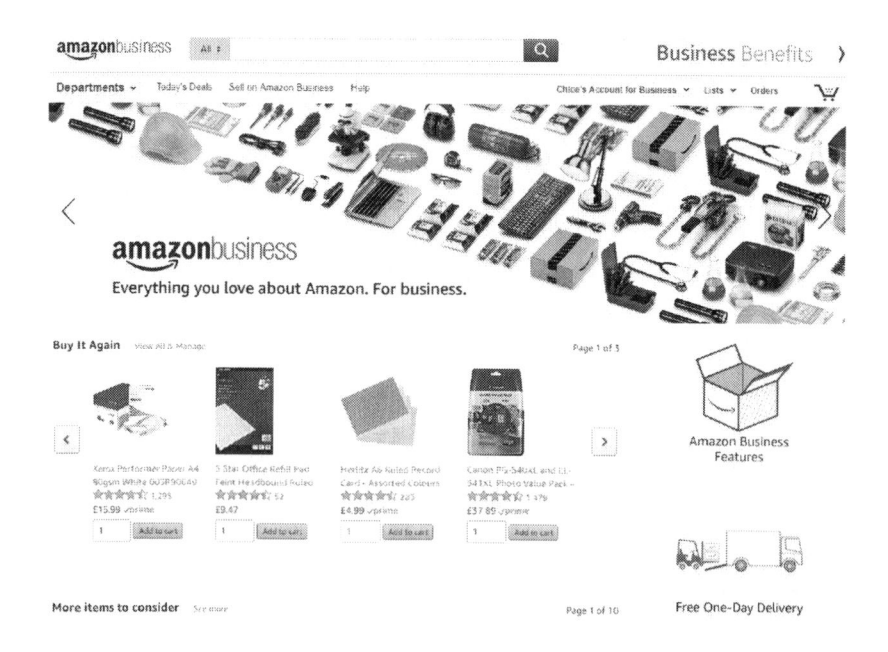

Reason 3: Your Customers Want It

Of course, it's one thing to make the decision based on trends across the whole B2B world or within your own market, but what about trends within your own business?

What do your customers want from you? Are they already asking for an online ordering portal?

When we get into the type of eCommerce site you're going to need, one of the recommendations will be to ask the customers what they would find most useful. Before that though, why not find out if your customers want it?

Every business is different, so you should base any decision of this magnitude more heavily on what your customers say, than on the big industry stats I've shared above.

Run a survey to find out if your customers want an eCommerce ordering option. How do they want to order from you and manage their account[15]?

Once you have the results, analyse them to find out not just if your customers want it, but also which customers want to order online – is it the biggest customers? The smallest customers? Or all of them? This will have a big impact on what you build and how you market it both internally and externally. We'll cover more on this in Stage 2.

Reason 4: Pressure from Within the Business

From my discussions with B2B manufacturers and wholesalers over the years, the final catalyst to launching an eCommerce site for B2B customers usually comes from within the business, whether that's financial, the team or something else. You can't afford to ignore internal pressures.

From the team

The internal pressure to build eCommerce into a B2B business can come from almost anywhere:

- **Customer feedback** harvested by the customer service team, or sales team: "The customers want to order online, help me help them".

---

15 You can access my survey template for this, which you can copy and use for surveying your customers, and recommended systems to run the survey on, via eCommerceMasterPlan.com/freeb2b

- **The Sales team**: "If only we had an online ordering system I could focus my effort on the big accounts and let the little ones sort themselves out. Overall I'll make a bigger bonus and you'll get more sales".

- **The Warehouse**: "Mondays would be so much easier if customers could place orders over the weekend. Then we wouldn't have to wait until lunchtime for the sales team to transfer the emails and voicemails that have come in into the system. We could get packing and despatching straight away".

- **Marketing**: "If we had an online product catalogue and ordering system, we could do much more interesting marketing – and make a bigger contribution to sales".

Financial

eCommerce will Increase Sales:

- **Increase sales from existing customers**: Given it's easier to buy, you should see additional orders from existing customers.

- **Gather sales from new customers**: They can find you and buy from you all online, without any of your team having to do a thing.

- **Open up a new target market**: You can add those whose potential annual purchase value is too low to have a sales rep dedicated to them, but who can buy from you online at a profit.

eCommerce will lower costs.

The human sales channel remains one of the most costly, but also the most effective. Migrating order taking to an automatic online system will remove some of the most low-value work from your team. This gives you the opportunity to either:

- Reduce headcount/hours and directly save money.
- Redeploy headcount into higher value areas:
    - Better relationships with highest-value customers.
    - Outbound calls to generate more sales and check on customer satisfaction.
    - Website Live Chat management on the website (this is a sales channel).

Interestingly, the majority of our case studies and research interviewees have actually increased sales team numbers since adding eCommerce to their business. And none had cut headcount as a result of the change. So, you'll probably find you're redeploying people, and improving cost per order.

BUT don't go thinking that moving into eCommerce won't add costs to the business.

You will need to invest in the website, and in marketing activity to both migrate customers to it and keep them buying from you. Plus, you'll need lots of man-hours to populate it with products and keep it up-to-date, and it certainly doesn't eradicate customer-service needs.

Why Should You Add a B2B Ecommerce Operation to Your Business and Work to Make It a Success?

Your Customers. Current and Future.

And, of course, profit.

Before you move on to Stage 2:

What do you think?

Is it clear that eCommerce will be a benefit for you?

Do your customers want it?

Does the team want it?

Jot down your thoughts. And answer these 2 questions:

1. Should B2B eCommerce be part of your business / the business you work for?

    Yes   No

2. When should it be a part of your business / the business you work for?

    Last year(!)   Now   Next Year   5 years' time

If no – feel free to stop reading!

If yes – whatever the timescale – you need to read on, because the time to tackle the next Stage is now.

Notes

3 Case Study: Upgrade Bikes

'What's going to help our B2B customer sell more?'

UPGRaDe

shop.upgradebikes.co.uk

UPGRADE BIKES DESIGNS, manufactures and wholesales bikes and bike parts, specialising in products for off-road and adventure biking with a global turnover well in excess of 7-figures.

Over the years, they've become experts in building a brand in the cycling world, so that sales to the B2C customer just grow and grow (all sold by their B2B customers to the end user). So now, as well as wholesaling their own DMR and Kinesis products, they also wholesale on behalf of another 20 bike part & accessories manufacturers both in the UK and overseas.

Their success is based on the success of their B2B Customers – so anything Upgrade Bikes can do to help them sell more, they do.

The Customer

The majority of Upgrade Bikes customers are specialist cycle retailers, one-off physical stores serving the cycling fanatics in their area. They also sell to the huge retailers in their space – Halfords, Wiggle, Chain Reaction, etc.

Quite a diverse set of needs! Not all the larger retailers use the eCommerce site, and they continue to have a traditional buyer-supplier relationship. Large retailers also receive a lot of marketing support from Upgrade Bikes.

However, those national chains where stock is ordered at the store level do use the website, which has been modified to give them a PO number checking and authorising system.

UK B2B sales are split 1/3 via the website, 2/3 via the account managers who look after the big stores.

They also serve B2C consumers online, but via a limited stock range.

The Websites

They've evolved from doing everything offline, to having 4 transactional websites. Although three of those exist to sell to the B2C customer, every single site exists to help their wholesale (B2B) customers sell more.

- Shop.upgradebikes.co.uk – The B2B eCommerce site. Exists to serve their B2B customers.

- Outlet.upgradebikes.co.uk – A B2C eCommerce site. Exists to sell demo stock (that used by the press to test the products), and small parts for all the brands they represent (e.g. replacement handle bars, or springs and clamps).

- DMRBikes.com
    - A B2C eCommerce site. Selling the small parts range for the DMR brand.
    - PLUS, the marketing content that builds the brand, serving as the centre for social media, news, press, product information, and of course their sponsored athletes.

- KinesisBikes.co.uk
    - A B2C eCommerce site. Selling the small parts range for the Kinesis brand.
    - PLUS, the marketing content that builds the brand, serving as the centre for social media, news, press, their sponsored athletes, and even a "Dealer of the Month" section.

Having a combined B2C and B2B eCommerce store was never a consideration, as they needed to serve such different purposes.

Plus, the level of pricing complexity on the B2B site does slow things down a bit – and adding a consumer dimension to that would just have slowed the system down for everyone.

Product Decisions

Upgrade Bikes use their B2C consumer-facing platforms to support their B2B customers by building the brand value and marketing the products. AND by giving the consumer somewhere to get the little parts that they need to maintain the products they've bought. This is because the majority of their wholesale customers don't want to stock every last spring option! So, the B2C Customer can get the product they need, and the B2B Customer can focus on selling the high-value products.

Yes, that means that on the DMRBikes website, you CAN NOT buy the full range, or even the headline/bestselling products. They are ONLY available through the companies that Upgrade Bikes wholesales too.

Clever, eh?

It's clear, easy to understand, and keeps everyone happy and working to the same goal – selling as much product to B2C consumers as possible.

B2B eCommerce Site Evolution

Upgrade Bikes took the decision to move their B2B sales online because it was the way their industry was going – their competition were already going there, and the customers were starting to expect it.

They spent two years trying to build the site they needed with a general site builder, but the pricing and speed just never worked. Their pricing is more complex than some because they have discounts by brand (they sell 22 brands in total) as well as by line, as well as dealer rates and special offers.

Once they moved to a specialist B2B agency (Aspidistra), everything moved quickly and they've never looked back.

Not one customer who was asked to start ordering online complained about the change.

Not one member of the team was cut because B2B customers were now ordering online.

2 things which the B2B eCommerce site has been able to do which you might not have considered:

1. The product information from the site is provided as a feed to all B2B customers, meaning that all product information is always accurate and of high quality, wherever it appears.

2. They've recently built a very cool returns processing site feature to manage warranty claims before the consumer has even put the item in the post. It's made a huge difference in the business; the warranty claims manager's job changed from spending the whole day dealing with non-stop phone calls, to just making the occasional outbound call.

STAGE TWO

Getting Everyone and Everything Ready

MANY A BUSINESS just dives straight into briefing and building the website – but there's a lot to consider before you do that. Things that will impact the website itself, and that need to be considered to make the project a success.

A survey of 100 US B2B eCommerce firms asked them to identify the three most critical factors in the successful implementation of their core eCommerce solution. The top 3 were:

- Successfully defining goals and objectives (56%).
- Involving users throughout the process to ensure the solution would meet end-user needs (46%).

- Engaging a knowledgeable system integrator/eCommerce consultant (46%)[16].

This Stage will show you how to manage these three factors in your eCommerce solution implementation project.

Another Business Model

Adding an eCommerce operation to any business is not a decision to take lightly because starting to serve your B2B customers via an eCommerce system is going to fundamentally change your business.

Serving customers online is a totally different business model than serving customers one-on-one. So, you need to be ready to add that new complexity into the business – it will affect how everyone spends their day.

Any eCommerce B2B site is about streamlining the order-placing process so that it requires less human input and becomes easier and more convenient for your customers.

It means that much of what your team currently does now needs to be done by the site and systems.

Things like:

- Product information, such as pictures and descriptions.
- Pricing and discounts.

---

16   B2B Execs Estimate 31% of E-Commerce Revenue to be Incremental, May 2014 (Marketing Charts) www.marketingcharts.com/industries/retail-and-e-commerce-42938

- Orders that will hit the system out of hours, so stock needs to be accurate and update itself.
- Credit checks.
- Invoice creating.
- Usual purchase habits.

The roles of your team will change too:

- **Sales team:** It will focus on new business and cross sell, rather than just get the order.
- **Call centre:** Less order taking, with more help and advice.
- **Warehouse:** It comes in every morning to find orders that need processing straight away.

There is much you need to get straight before you even think about Googling "B2B eCommerce site builder".

4 The Objectives

JUST WHY DOES your business need an eCommerce ordering channel for B2B customers?

Having a clear objective was the most important critical success factor in the marketingcharts.com survey. Here's some of the common objectives:

- Maintain/Increase sales from existing customers because:
    - The customers want it.
    - We have one big customer who uses an archaic EDI (Electronic Data Interchange) system and we need a new online solution for them.
    - We have won a contract to supply a new customer and having an online ordering system is a requirement.
    - Our customers want to be able to place orders when the call centre is shut.

- Attract new customers because:
  - 1 in 3 of the new accounts we fail to get say lack of online ordering was a key reason for picking the competition.
  - Our competitors don't offer it and we want to be first to seize the competitive advantage.
  - Our key competitor has launched an eCommerce site.
  - Younger customers won't deal with us because we aren't online.
  - We regularly get contacted by smaller retailers who we'd love to supply, but can't profitably supply via our current manual sales channels.
- Cut costs because:
  - The cost of doing business face-to-face (travel, staff) is just too high.
  - Of human error – too often a customer gets a better deal than they should, costing us margin.
  - We want to scale back our catalogue production.

Growing revenue is the goal of 4 out of 5 projects, with cost saving the goal half of the time, and competitive advantage just 37% of the time.[17]

Side benefits might include:

---

17   B2B Execs Estimate 31% of E-Commerce Revenue to be Incremental, May 2014 (Marketing Charts) http://www.marketingcharts.com/industries/retail-and-e-commerce-42938

- A product information feed that can be sent out to all the customers to make it really easy for them to keep their own websites up to date.

- The possible inclusion of stock information will enable your customers to offer a wider range than they have the space/can afford to stock now. E.g., their website says despatch within 3 days, which gives them time to order from you, and then send on to the customer.

  (You could also use this for direct despatch if you wanted...)

In identifying YOUR objectives, make sure you're talking to people throughout your business (HR, Sales, Finance, IT, Marketing). And if you wear all those hats, think of it from each angle.

But be careful not to try to deliver on every possible one. Identify the most important 1-3, and then make sure everyone understands the chosen objectives and why they've been selected. It's important to create clarity as to the core purpose of the B2B eCommerce site.

Who's the Customer?

Who is the site for? It might not be for all your customers; for some of them, you may want to keep that exclusive one-to-one relationship (usually the biggest).

This might mean it's for all your customers except for three specific ones.

You may want to build it for all your customers who order up to X times per year, or spend between £Y and £Z per year with you.

Even if you want all customers to use it, it is still worth being clear about which customer group it is most important for and is being designed to satisfy.

That decision is usually based on profitability and customer interest: Which customers want the website option, or which do you expect not to lose any sales from if they switch over? Which are too valuable to give up the personal touch?

And are there customer groups that you've lost or never targeted that you feel you could bring in once you have the eCommerce option?

Of course, just because the customers are ordering online doesn't mean you're not allowed to speak to them!! You might still want to visit them once a year (rather than 3 times a year), or give them a call now and then, send them a catalogue, or invite them to a drinks reception at your annual trade show.

Write down who this target customer group is.

Then have a chat with some of them. Do they like the idea? What does it need to do to make it work for them[18]?

Does what you learn fit with your objectives?

If there's a massive mismatch, you're going to need to revisit the whole idea of this project. But it's more likely that you'll gain some great ideas for the site, and how to market it to the customers before it's live — and once it's live.

---

18   You can download a list of questions to ask your customers via eCommerceMasterPlan.com/freeb2b

5 Team Impact: Getting Them Ready

By now you should be pretty clear on why the site is needed, which customers it will serve, and how it's going to do that.

But what about your team?

This is a massive change for them, even if you have no plans to make any cuts to headcount. It's going to fundamentally change their day-to-day activity, and change usually makes us scared and nervous.

Your team will need reassurance about what this means for them. Hopefully some of the case studies in this book and on the podcast will help you to reassure them.[19]

---

19 You'll find the case studies in Chapters 3,8,12 and 16. A full list of our B2B podcast interviews is available via:
eCommerceMasterPlan.com/freeb2b

The Sales Team

They will feel the biggest impact from this change, and the most anxiety about it too, as they worry about what it means for their bonuses and jobs.

Overall, a website should make their jobs easier and make it easier for them to increase their bonuses because it gives them more time to spend on finding and converting new customers. But that might not be their assumption when they first hear the news.

I suggest you start by finding out what they're worried about. Expect to get questions like these:

- Do they still have a job? — the day the site goes live, a year later?
- Do they still get a bonus? And how is it going to be calculated?
- How is their work rhythm going to change? Do they spend 4 days a week on the road now, and that's going to change to only 4 days a month?
- Will they still have a company car/laptop/mobile/expense account?
- What if the website screws everything up — and it's not their fault. Is their bonus protected?
- Are they still going to trade shows?

Make sure they understand that this is a move to increase sales, profitability, and security for the whole business. And that it will enable them to spend more time on their key clients and growing their client list.

The Call Centre Team

Assuming the sales team are out on the road, you've probably got someone in the office picking up the calls / faxes / emails from customers and the sales team – dealing with their queries and processing the orders.

They're going to have similar fears to the Sales team, and they may assume that a self-service website will mean they have nothing to do all day.

Explain that they're going to be key in helping the customers migrate, and that you expect there will still be plenty of questions about products and deliveries, and the occasional order coming in too.

You may want to outline potential opportunities for them – after all, you'll probably be adding a Live Chat that will need to be monitored, more emails, new customer enquirers, and you'll need someone to help create customer service content for the website too.

The Marketing Team

This could go one of two ways! They might be very excited about the prospect of helping drive sales directly online with lots of exciting new marketing methods. OR they may be afraid of the changes and worried the whole venture is just going to up their workload.

Be ready to deal with both options, and be sure to harness their help, as you will need them working on the launch plans.

The IT Team

Just like with the Marketing Team your discussions with the IT team could go one of two ways! They may be eager to actively help you get the integrations just right, or they may declare it a non-IT project.

Depending on your business either of these can be the right way forward! You don't have to get them actively on board if it's not the right thing for the project.

New Roles

Running an eCommerce website means you're going to need some new roles covered. These may be taken on by the existing team, or you may need to hire someone.

The biggest and most important is site merchandiser.

A site merchandiser is responsible for making sure the website is correct and up-to-date from day to day – that every product is there, that stock is accurate, that any promotions are communicated and working accurately. So in January, the homepage doesn't feature Christmas.

I've outlined the key teams who will be affected, but you need to speak to every team, and be ready to deal with their fears and listen to their input.

Be prepared for some of the team to not be ready to adapt to this new world. In which case, support them as much as you can and help them find new positions within your business, or elsewhere. Then, find the right person to replace them.

Throughout these conversations, you will probably learn things that impact on what you need from the site, which is another good reason to do this upfront.

Make sure you make a note of the feedback too.

How to Facilitate These Conversations

Unless you have a huge team (over 30), I'd suggest starting off with a meeting of everybody to run through the big picture. That way, everyone gets the same message and the big questions can be dealt with in one go.

Then meet with each person/each team separately to dive into their key concerns and what they would like to see the site deliver.

Do You Need to Hire The Skills and Knowledge in?

46% of B2B eCommerce firms named 'engaging a knowledgeable systems integration/eCommerce consultant' as one of the three most critical factors in the successful implementation of their eCommerce project.[20]

eCommerce is a whole different skill set so to bring into your team someone who has done this type of project before should help you avoid the pitfalls and make the whole project run more smoothly and more successfully. You may want to hire a full time eCommerce Manager, or engage the services of a consultant.

If the systems integration is the side of the project that has you most worried there are some fantastic consultants available who specialise in just this area. If your team needs an integration skills boost I'd recommend a consultant rather than a full time employee, as once it's set up you'll have little need for their skills and your team and site builders will have picked up enough to keep things working well.

---

20   B2B Execs Estimate 31% of E-Commerce Revenue to be Incremental, May 2014 (Marketing Charts) www.marketingcharts.com/industries/retail-and-e-commerce-42938

6 What You Need to Have Ready Before Your Site Can Be a Reality

WHILST THE CREATION of a website is obviously essential to starting to sell via eCommerce, there are a few things you need to have ready before that site can be launched.

Once you have your team on board, it is time to start making sure everything else is ready to go eCommerce.

Have a think through the systems and processes within the business. Is each ready to cope with, or provide or integrate to deal with:

- Customers placing orders 24/7?
- All product information being available 24/7, including stock availability?

- Accurately servicing customers via an automated system without constant manual activity?

Some systems you identify will need to be tweaked internally to become ready for eCommerce. To solve other systems issues, it will be about making sure it's possible for the new site to make sure it can fit your needs.

Remember to include this second group in the site brief you create (we'll cover that in Stage 3).

Below, I run you through some of the key areas you may need to get ready.

Pricing

Whichever site structure you chose, it's essential that it presents the right price to each customer, every time.

Getting the pricing right is often the most complex part of a B2B website build, if not for the site builders, then for whoever in your team is responsible for making sure the right pricing information is fed into the system.

Sometimes, like our case study Gloveman[21], that might mean a unique price list for every customer. But not every site system can handle that. And it's a lot of work to keep it all updated, even when integrated.

---

21 You can find the Gloveman Case Study in Chapter 12.

For many, therefore, it means streamlining your account pricing options, like Upgrade Bikes[22] — one pricing structure for all Resellers and one for all Pro-Shops.

A streamlined price list makes setting up and checking and maintaining the website a lot easier. It will also make customer liaison a lot simpler for your team — there are fewer pricing anomalies to remember!

Is it time to streamline your pricing?

If you currently have a bespoke pricing option for every single customer, I highly advise that you consider a streamlined pricing structure even if only for some of your customers.

Why should you streamline?

- Each extra pricing dimension slows your website down because it is another call on the database, another process for the server to run. The slower the website, the fewer orders will be placed.

- It will make the site set up much easier. Rather than creating one pricing structure per customer, you'll be creating maybe 4 or 5 pricing structures. That massively lowers the potential for error.

- It also greatly reduces the pre-live testing. For each pricing structure, you'll need to test to be sure it works accurately on both mobile and desktop. Not just once, but multiple times as the site develops during the build.

---

22   You can find the Upgrade Bikes case study in Chapter 3.

- Once you're up online, you'll have the ability to tweak promotions and offer new promotions. That's a lot easier to do if you only have to check how it impacts 5 pricing structures rather than 100s.

The only right answer with pricing is what's best for your customers and business.

If you aren't going to streamline, make sure you pick a site builder who can integrate with the price structure on your existing system. A good integration will cut out most of the headaches for you.

The system should also be able to handle override discounts, minimum order quantities, and any finance options you offer.

Delivery[23]

Often an offline B2B delivery is calculated for each order individually. That is not good in the world of eCommerce.

Delivery uncertainty and unexpected charges are the number one reason customers fail to check out. (that includes time, as well as price).

Can you streamline your delivery information so that it's easy to understand AND doesn't have to be calculated offline?

---

23   Done well, delivery can both win you new customers, and get you repeat purchases. Find out more about that in my book "eCommerce Delivery: How your Delivery Strategy Can Increase Your Sales" available via eCommerceMasterPlan.com/books

Ideally, you want to get to a standard price and speed per order: e.g., £5 per delivery, all orders processed next working day. If your shipping fees need to factor in weight or location, then you should be able to set the criteria in the website so the correct fee appears in the checkout. If you feed in weight info, you can usually build an algorithm that builds the postage price as you go.

Of course, there may be exceptions to the rule — those customers who flatly refuse to ever pay postage, or a customer where 79 of their locations qualify for free shipping and the 80th doesn't, so you've extended the free P&P to the 80th. If delivery charges and services are an area you use to negotiate with customers, make sure custom delivery options can be set for each customer.

Stock information

Having clear delivery information so the customer knows when they will receive the goods is useless if it's not clear what products are in stock, and when those that are out of stock will be back in.

For a B2C consumer, a product not being immediately available is an annoyance; for a B2B customer it can have an immediate impact on their profits and customer service. If the customer wants it and you can't provide it, you're going to lose out as the customer orders from a competitor.

So, make sure it's clear on your website whether products are in stock, and if they're not. when the product will be back in.

£99.01 ex VAT

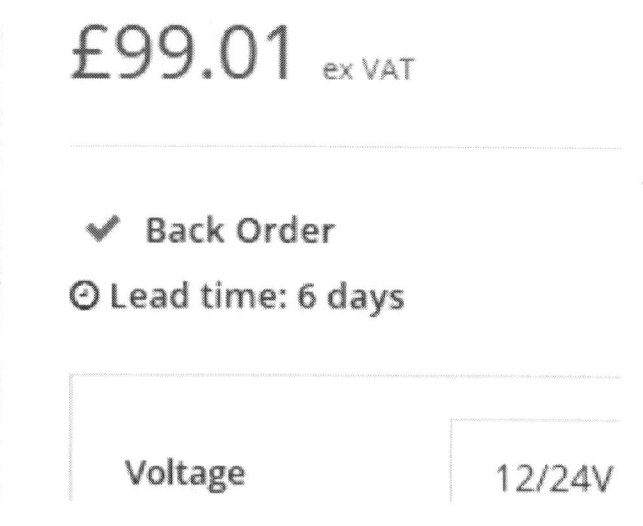

✔ Back Order
⏱ Lead time: 6 days

| Voltage | 12/24V |

Of course, if your products are ALWAYS in stock – then make that clear too!

Product Information

You can't escape the need for product information on an eCommerce site. At a minimum, every product will need:

- A name
- A unique reference number (usually a SKU code)
- An image
- Copy and information that the customer needs to know before purchasing

⭐ Product on Promotion until 31st August 2017

Mr Kipling Eton Mess Tart
6pk × 1

Log in to buy

Product:	Pastry cases with a layer of plum and raspberry jam (8%) and vanilla flavour sponge (18%), topped with pink fondant icing (30%) and meringue pieces (3%).
RSP:	£1.00
POR:	15.00%
Pack Size:	6pk
Pack Quantity:	6 x Tarts
Product Code:	347091
VAT Code:	Exempt
Brand:	Mr Kipling
Product Category:	Bread & Cakes > Cakes > Kipling Cadbury & Lyons

Description | Ingredients/Nutrition | Other Info

- 100% natural flavours & no artificial colours
- No hydrogenated fat

#exceedinglygood
@mrkiplingcakes

Product Marketing
A twist on our cherry Bakewell classic - A decadent tart tasting of a favourite summer pudding- Eton Mess!

Brand Marketing
Mr Kipling, what a lovely fellow. A proper gentleman with a belief that if something is worth doing, it is worth doin true attention to detail, it is no wonder that Mr Kipling is one Britain's favourites†
All proudly made in Britain. Did you know that last year, Mr Kipling baked and sold over 134 million boxes of cak
† IRI Grocery Outlets, 52 w/e 28 January 2017, Ambient Packaged Cake
†† IRI Grocery Outlets, 52 w/e 31 December 2016, Mr Kipling Cake

Have you tried Mr Kipling's Strawberry Cheesecake Whirls?
Another exceedingly good cake inn our summer range

[if you need this much information just for some cakes….]

If you already have a B2C eCommerce site, or a catalogue, then this process won't be so hard, since you can start with the product information you already have.

However, it's still going to take time to get all the information, for every product, right for the B2B website.

Ideally for Search Engine Optimisation (and because the customer wants to know different things), you'll be using different copy for each product on your B2B site.

Ideally you want copy that's unique to both the product page (so don't use the same description for two products even if the only difference is the colour) and unique to the B2B eCommerce website.

Transferring data from a catalogue:

- Often, text descriptions get edited down to fit into the page. You really want the longer pre-edited version.

- In the catalogue, you may have grouped a number of products together (all the colours of a t-shirt, all the sizes of a screw) with one description. That's (probably) not going to be the same way you group them on the website, so you'll need to duplicate and edit some descriptions to fit.

- You may have products that you sell that aren't in the catalogue. If you want to sell those on the website, you need all the same information for them too.

Transferring data from a B2C eCommerce site:

- In many cases, your B2B customer doesn't need all the same information as a B2C customer — they don't need the flowery copy that brings emotion to the buying process! So, you may want to change the copy to be more B2B-friendly.

- The B2B customers have different information needs, too. They are usually buying product in multiples, or by the box, not as single units. So how big is each box? How many units are in it? What's the minimum purchase volume? Are there volume discounts?

- Some information will be the same — the product image, the product name, the SKU. So, if you can export a spreadsheet of all this, it is a great starting point.

Manufacturers information

If you buy your products in from another business, they may be able to supply you with this product content. That's a great place to start from, but be ready to improve upon it if your customers need you to.

And if you're hoping to use SEO to attract new customers to your website at some point, you're going to want to make your product information your own so you don't get penalised for having duplicate content on the website (content that's also on your suppliers' website). Search engines like Google will penalise you for that.

General product information tips

When deciding on your product names, make sure when a customer is looking through them that they help them work out what's different about each product. So, if you've separated the colours of a t-shirt into different items on the website, make sure the name includes the colour each time.

With product content, include the information the customer wants to know. What do they need to know before they're going to buy? What questions do they usually ask when ordering? For the first time? For the 10th time?

Your product content will constantly evolve based on what you learn from your customers about how they want to buy from you online.

You don't have to have it all perfect on day 1! (We'll cover the continuous optimisation of your website in Chapter 18.)

Maybe you aim to get one category done per month, or the top 10% of sellers done first, then work your way through the rest of the list.

Or go live with the same manufacturer information as everyone uses on day 1, and improve it for 10 products each week until everything is done.

Feel free to tackle this, and the product images, in phases if it makes it possible/easier.[24]

---

[24] In my podcast interview with Rob Boyle of Homespares, we discuss how he's taken this approach in launching their B2C eCommerce site. Find that interview at eCommerceMasterPlan.com/podcast

Product Images

I've split product images out into their own section because this is a whole other set of challenges!

Images are super-important to reassure customers that they are selecting the right item when buying online. So you need accurate images of each product you're selling. You might want both images of the final product AND images of how the pack that sits on the retailer's shelf looks.

MORE VIEWS

And yes, I said images. Frequently you're going to need more than one image, if only to illustrate the product from different angles, or show fine detail.

In the last few years, it has become considerably cheaper and easier to manage the photography process in house, especially if all your products are pretty small.

- Many mobile phones now have enough photography power for product shots.

- Lightboxes (literally a lit-up box in which you place a product to shoot it) are very easy to get hold of.

If you're going to do this in house, the one thing I recommend spending the cash on is the lighting, because the right lighting setup will make the whole thing so much easier. Get a local photographer (the one who does the school photos maybe?) to come in and advise you on what equipment to buy to fit out your studio, and then help you set it all up. Dedicate some space to this; it's that important!

If you want to outsource it, there are many specialist product photographers out there. Find one who has experience with your product type. If you're selling widgets, you don't want a fashion photographer! If you're selling fashion, you want someone who has experience sourcing and working with models, as well as the cut-out shots.

Logistics play quite a big part in this too; you must physically get each product to the photography studio (whether in house or outsourced) and back into stock again. Often not a simple task...

If you currently produce another website featuring your product, or a catalogue, this process should be a bit easier. But double, double check you do have photos of everything.

If you are buying your product from someone else before you sell it, they may be able to provide you with product images – but double check to be sure they're all there! And you may not be happy with the quality, so you may still need to take some yourself.

Getting the photos ready for the website

- They all need to be the same ratio — usually square.
- They all need to be the same size (and you may need to create 3 sizes of each one – thumbnail, product page, and zoom). And they should be the proper resolution to display crisply, but not require a file size that makes your site load slowly.
- If you have more than one image per product, you'll need to decide which one is the main image, and which ones are options the customer can chose to view if they want to.
- You need to tie each image to each product. That's either done by uploading images individually to each product listing, OR by adopting a naming convention that means you can bulk upload and the site will know which images goes with which product — E.g., "skucode.jpg". Your site builder will be able to advise you how it works on their system.

For the eCommerce MasterPlan Podcast, I managed to get an interview with Gabrielle O'Hare, the Content Controller at Argos, who manages a photography and video studio of 83 people! Have a listen to episode 109 at eCommerceMasterPlan.com/podcast for more information on how to get your product imagery just right.

Specialist Product Information

If you are selling more technical products, there may be additional information your customers need before they are able to make the decision to buy. Things like specification sheets or CAD files.

Festo Mini Semi-Auto Filter Regulator & Lubricator Set G1/8 — FESTO

Downloads
- Festo 159608.pdf

Delivery Information

If you want the customers to have self-service access to these on the new site, then that must go into the tender, and you'll need to get all the files ready.

I'd strongly advise making sure you have those files for EVERYTHING before you launch, because consistent product information is important to build trust with your customers —trust in both your business and your website.

Product Structure

This is working out what counts as a product on the website, and what counts as a product option.

Let me explain with an example.

If you are selling a polo shirt "The Polo Shirt" that's available in 10 colours and each colour is available in 5 sizes and you put it all on one product page, there are 3 different dropdowns the customer needs to pick from before they can hit the buy button. They need to choose a colour, a size, and a quantity. That's pretty complex for a consumer buying one t-shirt, let alone a retailer buying multiples across sizes and colours.

Better to have 10 product pages, one for each colour: "The Polo Shirt Blue", "The Polo Shirt Green" etc. Then the customer only has to make two choices — size and quantity. Plus, as there are only two variables, it's probably going to be possible to enable them to put in a quantity for each size and hit buy, which makes it really easy for them to order in bulk.

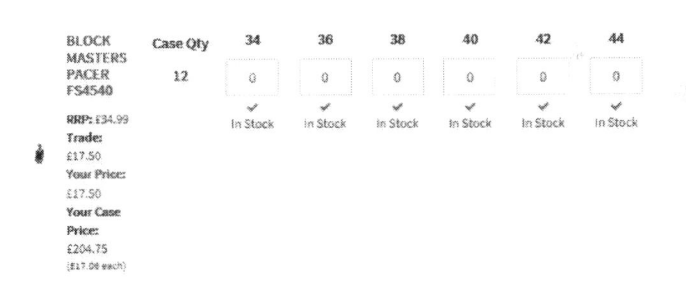

BLOCK MASTERS PACER FS4540	Case Qty	34	36	38	40	42	44
	12	0	0	0	0	0	0
RRP: £34.99		In Stock	In Stock	In Stock	In Stock	In Stock	In Stock
Trade: £17.50							
Your Price: £17.50							
Your Case Price: £204.75 (£17.06 each)							

ADD TO BASKET

So how do you need to structure your products on the website to make it as easy as possible for the customer to buy?

This might even mean combining some products — e.g., a machine, together with its consumables.

Customer Database or CRM (Customer Relationship Management System)

This is the system where you manage your customer's information (contact details etc) and their accounts (invoices, credit limits, pricing).

What you need to do with it in order to be ready depends on how integrated you want it to be with your website. If you want to provide each customer with a full account management hub on the site, then you need to be sure everything is on your system that should be for every customer AND that there's nothing there that shouldn't be.

If you have a sales person who keeps creating invoices in the wrong account, now is the time to tidy it all up.

You may also want to identify dormant and active accounts so you have a clearer idea of how much data will be integrated.

If you're just putting up a site to manage smaller customers with a simple discount code, tidying up the CRM to get it ready for integration is much less important.

Marketing Plans and Budgets

Just putting the site live and hoping your customers will find it is a terrible idea.

You are going to have to make sure they know it exists and encourage them to try it out. Some of that will be done by the sales team, and some of that via your marketing activity.

Even if you're not planning on recruiting new customers via the website, you still need to be ready to market the website.

So, make sure all the "eCommerce Project Budget" isn't used up by the day it goes live; you need some budget for marketing.

As in the Gloveman case study (see Chapter 12), you may also choose to add some sales team incentives for getting customers to use the website.

We'll cover the marketing in detail in Stage 4.

7 B2B eCommerce Site Structure Options

THERE ARE CORE types of B2B eCommerce sites. The difference between them is all about how easy, or difficult, you make it to buy from you.

Working out which is the right one for your business is the first decision you need to make as you start building your B2B eCommerce operation.

Below are the key options with their pros and cons, followed by some of the website spinoffs you might want to consider.

Open eCommerce Site

This is where you build a normal open eCommerce site (say on Shopify), and every product has one price.

Any different discount options are managed with voucher codes at the checkout, and every customer pays by credit card as they place their order.

Essentially, you're creating a 'normal' eCommerce site for your B2B customers to use.

This is most often used by businesses whose B2B customers behave in a very similar way to consumers — they are interior designers, jewellery designers, one-man-band builders, etc.

Pros for your customers:

- Full access to everything without having to remember a login.
- Quick and easy to use from the first visit.

Pros for your business:

- Low cost — Shopify starts at $29/m and is easy to build without any coding experience[25].
- You can manage every customer (B2B and B2C) with just one website.
- Great if your B2B customers act like consumers.

Cons:

- Can't handle complex pricing structures.
- Can't handle PO numbers or offline invoicing.

---

[25] We've negotiated a special discount on this — just go to eCommerceMasterPlan.com/shopify to access it

- exVAT pricing is complicated and not standard.

Examples:

- walcothouse.com: Curtain Pole suppliers to the interior designer market.
- beadsdirect.co.uk: Europe's number 1 bead and jewellery making supplier[26].

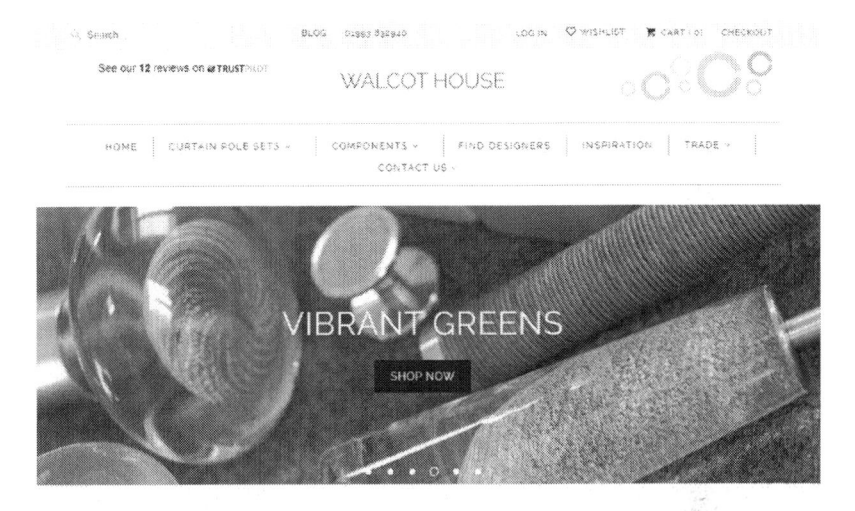

Shop Window With Trade Accounts Login

Think of this as like an eCommerce website with no buy buttons on display (sometimes the list price or RRP can be seen; sometimes there are no prices at all).

---

26 Hear about both these businesses on our podcast: eCommerceMasterPlan.com/podcast

Anyone can see your whole product range and how much a consumer should be able to buy the products for. But they can't even add to a basket, let alone check out.

In order to buy, the customer needs to have a login. You may choose to enable them to apply for an account on the website:

- With an algorithm automatically sorting those you want to have access from those you don't — e.g., a valid VAT number — you get 5% off RRP until someone properly vets you.

- Or they may need to fill in a form and wait for someone to get back to them.

Alternatively, you may not want to encourage, or take, applications online. But I do recommend you at least have your contact details so, if someone really wants an account, they can get in contact.

Pros for your customers:

- They can access product information without having to login. It's super quick for them to check the details. Think of it like a printed catalogue that's always up-to-date without prices.

- They can use the site (when they're not logged in) to guide their customers through any product they'll need to order in for them.

- The price they're going to pay is clear at every stage; they don't have to enter a code in the checkout to see it. It's there on the homepage, the product pages, and in the basket.

Pros for your business:

- A great replacement for that expensive big catalogue you've been producing.
- You are in control of who gets to buy from you.
- You have huge control over the pricing you set up for each account.
- The site can be customised to give each customer a unique buying experience (see the Gloveman VIP case study for more on this).
- New customers can research you and your products easily.

Cons:

- May frustrate B2C customers as they can't buy, so it's best to include a suppliers list.
- Anyone can see your full product catalogue.
- Much more complex to set up and manage.
- There are no off-the-shelf systems that can do this, so it's more expensive.
- The account application process is a barrier to new customers purchasing (although often a worthwhile one).

Examples:

- shop.upgradebikes.co.uk: Sells products for the cycle enthusiast; see our case study in Chapter 3.
- indanc.com: Sells pipes and valves; see the case study in Chapter 8.
- australisdistribution.com: Sells a range of beauty products.

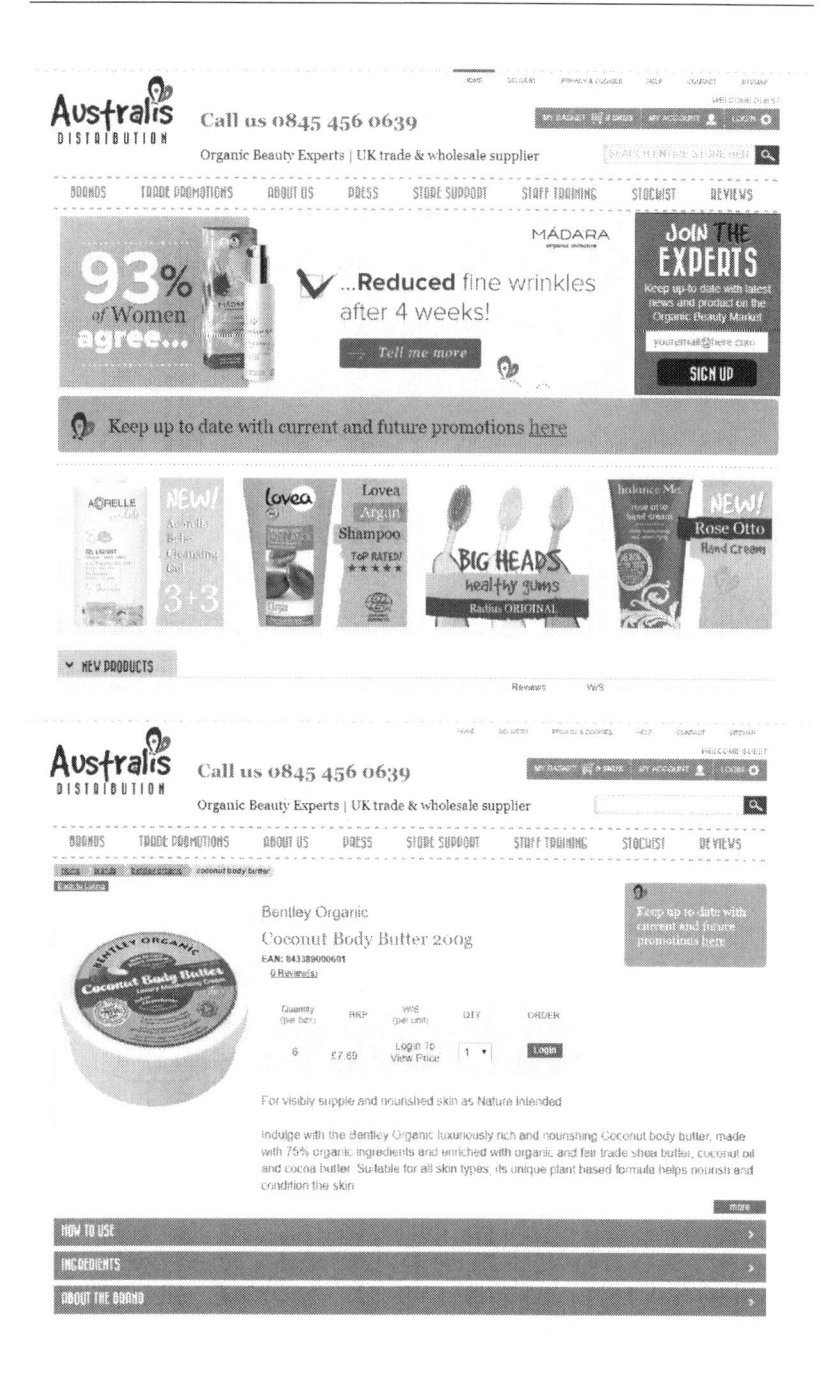

Rather than a buy button they have a "Login" link

Open eCommerce Site With Trade Accounts Login

For many businesses, if you've gone to the effort of the shop window options, why not sell from it to those who don't have a trade account?

This is very similar to the Shop Window with Trade Account Login option, only the site you get to before logging in has retail prices for each product and a fully working checkout. So anyone can buy from it.

The decision to put what is essentially a B2C eCommerce site live is not one to be taken lightly. So if you're considering this option, have a read of the bonus Chapter 18 about going B2C for all the pros and cons.

Examples:

- **screwfix.com:** Their main site supplies building materials to consumers and businesses alike, with trade accounts managed via a credit card system, and via separate sites ElecticFix and PlumbFix.

Closed Trade-only Portal

Once the B2B customer is logged in, this works just like the Shop Window with Trade Account option.

The different is that there is no shop window of your products. Before logging in, all that can be accessed is a homepage asking them to login. And maybe other information about your business.

Pros over the Shop Window with Trade Account:

- You are in complete control of your product content; only those with a login can see it.

Cons:

- Everything is behind the login, making it hard for prospective customers to research your business. Given 83% of B2B buyers prefer to research on the supplier's website, that could cost you new business[27].

Examples:

- Homespare.com: They actively direct people to the retail site if they want to get the products[28].

- Booker.co.uk: A UK cash-and-carry business.

---

27   B2B E-Commerce Statistics & Latest Trends 2017, Feb 2017 (Avatar) www.avatarsyndicate.com/inline/b2b-e-commerce-statistics-latest-trends-2017/

28   Hear more about Homespares on the podcast at: eCommerceMasterPlan.com/podcast

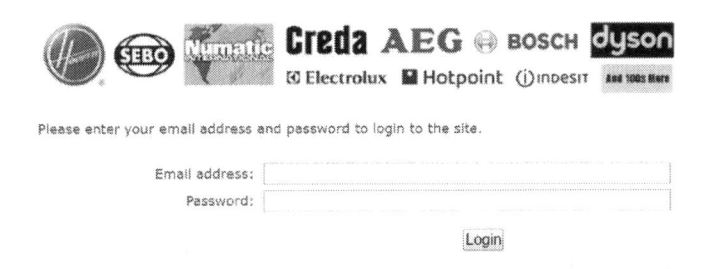

Take some time to work out exactly which of these is going to be right for your business. It's a fundamental, foundational decision that you really want to get right!

The case studies throughout this book should help you in making this decision too.

Website Spinoffs

Once you've gone to the trouble of getting all your product information into your website, there are a couple of things you might want to do with it to help your customers more, and increase sales.

A white label/distributor option

Once the product information is web-ready in one database, it can easily be used to create further websites.

A white label site is a website you provide to one of your B2B customers (so it's their branding and on their domain); they use it to sell the goods you supply them to their customers.

You keep the site and product information up-to-date, and ship the orders that come in.

Your customer does the marketing and drives the sales.

You might choose to give them the website, or charge them for it; usually that decision is based on volume of orders (surprise, surprise!).

This white-label model is the beating heart of some distributors' business models. Take a look at The Pharmacy Centre below. The primary selling method of their B2B customers is via the website that is provided for them by The Pharmacy Centre.

For other businesses, it is just a great way to help the customer out. Industrial Ancillaries (see our case study in Chapter 8) has used it to help their customers sell a wider range of stock options without having to buy and store it themselves.

If you think this might be part of your future, make sure you chose a website provider for your main eCommerce site who can easily roll out these white label sites for you. Doing this with a provider who's set up to do it will save you £10,000s per year in build and maintenance fees.

Pros for your customers:

- They get a website which is managed for them!
- They can better serve their customers, with larger product ranges.
- They can increase their sales.

Pros for your business:

- A great way to get your B2B customers to increase their sales, and therefore increase your sales.
- Your customers are accurately representing your products online.
- It ties them into you, rather than your competition. The only product they can put on the website is yours, and if they stop buying from you, they lose the website.

Cons:

- You have to be ready to ship all those consumer orders too.

- They might not be very good at marketing the website, so you get very few orders.

Examples:

- thepharmacycentre.com: Offers white-labelled e-pharmacy websites.

- Industrial Ancillaries: Uses this to help their customers sell more.

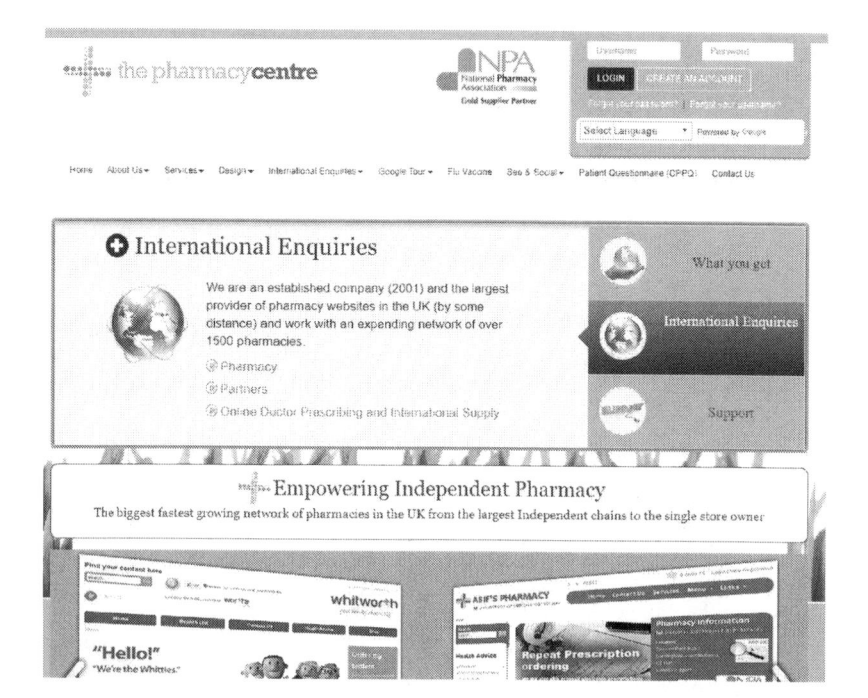

Full product feed

If your customers already have websites, or want to build their own, then this can be a great option.

You provide a feed of your product data — names, SKUs, images, descriptions, key information that they can import directly into their website.

This can be as simple as putting it onto a CD and posting it to them.

Or you can get it completely integrated into their website so that each time you improve something, or add a new product, the same change is made on their website.

Pros for your customers:

- They can easily put all your products on their website.

Pros for your business:

- Your customers are accurately representing your products online; no more bad descriptions, or terrible photos.

Cons:

- It doesn't help SEO, as it means there is duplicate content on everyone's website[29].

---

29   I'm not going to get into duplicate content here, but you can find the latest info on it via eCommerceMasterPlan.com/freeb2b

Example:

- **Upgrade Bikes** does this. Find more details in their case study in Chapter 3.

Hybrids/custom builds for customers

Once you start offering an online ordering process, you may find some customers need a level of customisation for it to work well for them.

Two of our case studies have created a custom check-out process to enable businesses with lots of sub-locations to manage the whole ordering process. In each case, when the sub-locations are about to place an order, it doesn't get processed until someone at head office has signed it off and applied a purchase order number. Head office can also amend or cancel the order. And everyone is kept in the loop throughout.

This makes the whole process much easier for everyone:

- The sub-location purchaser can place the order when it suits them, and (so long as it's all signed off) just wait for delivery.
- Head office has total visibility of and control over what's being spent.
- You get the order, but don't have to process it or ship until it's 100% going to be paid for.

Each of these systems will probably have an element of bespoke work in them, so be sure it's worth it before you put the time and money into building it out.

Again, if you think your current or future customers are going to want this, make sure the person you hire to build your main B2B eCommerce website can build these bespoke checkouts, for a reasonable price.

Pros:

- Ties the customer more deeply into you because your system fits with theirs.
- Should increase orders from that customer, as it becomes easier for them to use you than your competitors.

Cons:

- A lot of investment up front.

There is a lot to think about when it comes to the fundamental functionality of your eCommerce website, so don't rush choosing which option is right for you. And make sure any future functionality you're considering is possible with the company building your website.

For more, see the bonus chapter on What Successful Websites need.

Before You Move on to Stage 3:

Are you ready to start building your B2B eCommerce operation?

Jot down your thoughts and answer these questions:

1. Should B2B eCommerce be part of your business/the business you work for?

   Yes   No

2. When should it be a part of your business/the business you work for?

   Last year(!)   Now/Next Year   5 years' time?

If No, feel free to stop reading!

If Yes, whatever the timescale, here's a couple more questions to answer:

1. Are your project objectives clear?

   Yes   No

3. Are the teams ready?

   Yes   No

4. Are your systems and processes ready? OR do you know what you need to do to make them ready?

   Yes   No

5. Have you identified the right B2B site structure for your business?

   Yes   No

If you've answered No to any question, go and get that resolved before you start speaking to site builders.

If it's all Yes, you need to read on, because you're ready to start building that website, and make your B2B eCommerce dreams a reality!

Notes

8 Case Study: Industrial Ancillaries

'People still buy from people'

Indanc.com

INDUSTRIAL ANCILLARIES IS a family business founded in 1969, which Jamie Dennis took over from his stepfather in 2003. It's an engineer's merchant, selling the components that keep a factory going (tubes, fittings and valves). It was set up to serve the factories in the local Chesterfield area, but as many of the local factories closed down over the last 20 years, the business had to look farther afield.

They've become adept at adapting to the changing landscape, taking advantage of new trends and markets and identifying sectors where gas or liquid needs to be moved. They now serve everyone from hospitals and nuclear power stations to dentist's practices.

This expansion in customer markets has increased their SKU count (number of products) more than 20 times. They now have 35,000 items ready for next-day delivery from their 40,000 square feet of warehouse space.

Going eCommerce

Jamie takes great pride in their early adoption of technology. Their first site went live in the early 1990s, and they've been offering an eCommerce service for nearly 10 years.

For Industrial Ancillaries, a B2B eCommerce site was all about making sure there were no barriers to the customer being able to purchase, and to giving the customer the choice of how to buy.

Initially, eCommerce sales were slow, but they are now growing fast, especially as the younger 'millennial' generation starts taking over the purchasing roles within their customers' businesses.

The Role of the Product Catalogue

The catalogue remains a key part of the business that they have no intention of dropping; it's still the preferred research method for their older customers. And it's a really important way to build and maintain brand positioning and awareness. It is particularly important for maintaining sales of the product ranges for which they are not the sole UK distributors.

The production focus has switched to the website, so fewer manhours are put into the catalogue than the website. And despite the huge growth in SKUs, the catalogue has remained the same size.

The Industrial Ancillaries customer

The eCommerce site only serves the B2B customer; to access pricing and the checkout, you have to have an account.

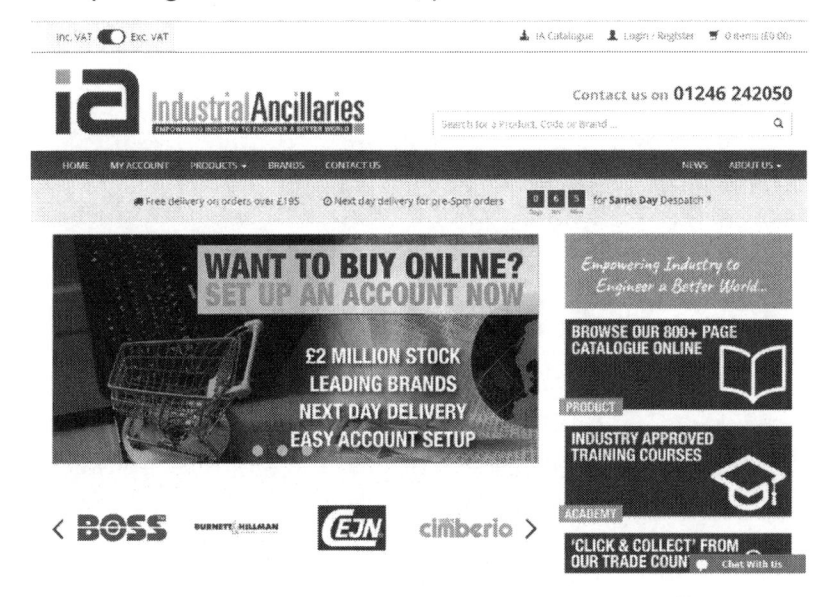

B2B2C – Helping the Industrial Ancillaries B2B Customer Serve Their B2C Customers

A few years ago, Industrial Ancillaries noticed a new opportunity.

Several of the smaller retailers they supplied products too were keen to offer the full range to their customers, but couldn't afford the cash flow or space to stock it all.

This presented a big opportunity, so Industrial Ancillaries created a B2C eCommerce website for each of those B2C customers who wanted one. This enabled the B2B customers a very easy way to increase their stock range, better serve their B2C customers, and increase sales. Very easy because the website and all product information is maintained by Industrial Ancillaries, as is the product despatching.

It becomes a really easy way for Industrial Ancillaries to help their retail customers increase their sales. Of course, it also creates another great reason for the retailer to keep buying from Industrial Ancillaries – switch supplier and lose your website.

Impact on the Sales Force

The growth of eCommerce in the business has made no impact on the size of the sales force at Industrial Ancillaries (in fact as this book goes to print they're actively hiring).

Every customer has access to buy via the website if they want it; it's just another tool to help get the order —a convenience order-taker.

But the website isn't as good at building a relationship, talking about new product launches, picking up feedback, or finding more ways to help the customer. So, the sales team remains a key part of the business, because talking with the customers remains a key activity.

The B2B eCommerce site is a really important tool for new customer acquisition too, because it's where new customers do a lot of their research —it's where they find you, and judge you. The first impression used to be the yellow pages advert; now it's the website.

STAGE THREE

Making the Website a Reality

Now that you are ready to expand into the eCommerce business model, it's time to get that website live, to make the whole idea a reality. This Stage is purely about getting the site live. So, we won't be going into how to optimise the site (see the bonus Chapter 17 on successful websites) or getting traffic and generating sales (see Stage 4!). I suggest you read those too before you embark on actually briefing your website(s).

The website is the most important part of any eCommerce business; it's what the customer interacts with to research, and place orders.

What sort of website do you need? How many do you need? One per brand or product line, or all in one? How do you get the right site built quickly and effectively?

Building and getting a site live usually takes at least three months, sometimes more than a year, and the costs can be huge once you build in what you must pay for the site, the impact that not having it has on sales, and the time it takes you to manage the project (time is money, after all).

Several of the B2B eCommerce businesses I've been chatting with during the researching of this book told me horror stories about the creation of their first eCommerce sites. Some recalled the launch of their new eCommerce route to market being held up by months, and in some cases years, because they chose the wrong company to build it, or the scope just kept changing.

Those are expensive delays; they're stopping your business from realising the benefits of allowing customers to order direct.

By taking on the advice in the rest of this Stage, you should be able to avoid such scenarios.

9 What Does the Website Need to Do?

ECOMMERCE IS ABOUT selling products online. Your website is responsible for displaying your products, getting the visitors to add those products to the basket, and also making sure they complete the order. If your website doesn't do its job, everything else in your business will be more difficult. Even if you have the best products and marketing in the world, you are not going to sell very much if your website isn't pulling its weight.

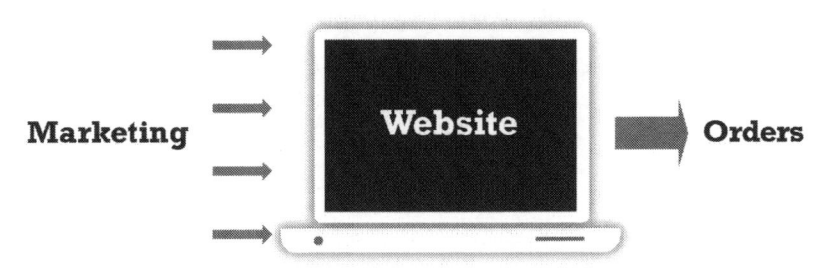

Marketing → Website → Orders

An eCommerce website is hard to get right because, in order get the orders placed, it should do a wide range of things, and the list increases all the time. It must:

- Showcase your products.

- Create/represent your brand. As your customers start buying online from you, the site is going to become their number 1, and possibly only, regular interaction with your brand.

- Support your marketing activity.

- Convert well – get customers to buy, both making it easy AND encouraging them.

- Capture customer information, to fulfil the orders and create new accounts.

- Deliver great customer service.

- Meet the legal criteria for selling online.

It's a real juggling act to get this right.

In Stage 2, we covered product information, product images, delivery, pricing and a few other areas. There are also some pieces of functionality you may want to consider, as they often make it easier for customers to order. Each of these is something that would be available to ALL customers, so they are part of the normal website, not a special option for one specific customer.

Which of these should be part of your B2B eCommerce website depends on how your customers are going to shop. So, some might be a yes for live, and others a potential future development.

Direct Order From Product Category

A B2B customer is likely to be buying several different SKUs and multiple quantities of each. Make it easy for them to do this by enabling them to set their quantity and add to the basket right on the product category page, rather than having to click into each individual product.

Easy Order Lists

SWCA24 - Cycle Computer - Wired (Box Qty: 200) £3.99
SWCA25 - Cycle Computer - Wireless (Box Qty: 200) £6.99
SWCA26 - Deluxe Cycle Computer - Wired (Box Qty: 200) £6.99
SWCA27 - Deluxe Cycle Computer - Wireless (Box Qty: 200) £8.99
SWRF1 - Red Reflector (Box Qty: 200) £1.10
SWCA5 - Bicycle Lighting Kit (Box Qty: 48) £1.56
SWCA7 - Bicycle Super Bright LED Light (Box Qty: 60) £2.99
SWCA14 - Rear Bike Light with Twin Lasers (Box Qty: 100) £2.50
SWCA19 - Bicycle Head Light (Box Qty: 100) £1.99
SWCA20 - Bicycle Rechargeable Rear Light (Box Qty: 100) £4.15
SWCA22 - Silicon Light (Box Qty: 240) £1.26
SWCRK2 - Bicycle Puncture Repair Kit (Box Qty: 30) £2.38
12v Travel Accessories
SWHD - 12v Hair Dryer (Box Qty: 24) £6.99
SWHS - Heated Hair Straighteners (Box Qty: 12) £5.50
SWK1 - Car Kettle 12v with Accessories (Box Qty: 20) £5.55
SWTF1 - Travel Flask (Box Qty: 48) £1.99
SWK2 - 12v Large Capacity Kettle (Box Qty: 12) £7.99
SWK3 - 24V Large Capacity Kettle (Box Qty: 20) £7.99
SWHE - 12v Water Heater Element (Box Qty: 100) £1.99
Add All to Basket
Please ensure you click 'Add All To Basket' before leaving this page

This takes ordering from the category to a whole other level!

This is a single page on your website where ALL products are listed, so the customer can select the quantity for each product they want in this order, and hit add to basket once.

This can turn into a problem rather than a benefit for customers if you have a very large number of products.

Upload Order by Spreadsheet

CSV Order Upload   +

	A	B
1	Stock Code	Qty
2	G20C-BST	2
3	G48-40RB	2
4	G24PP	5
5	G32T-BST	1
6	M120T-BST	3
7	BN6	7
8	G20PT	2
9	G16-12T-BST	6
10	G16-12S	10
11	G64E-BST	1
12	FL32-PN16/8	1

If your customers like to build their orders in a spreadsheet, or they have their own system which identifies what they need, then offering them the ability to upload their order as a spreadsheet would be a great piece of functionality to have on the website.

All they have to do is create a CSV file where column A is the SKU (or stock) code, and column B is the quantity they want.

Once this is uploaded to the website, they can see a confirmation of their order, including pricing, stock and delivery information before they place it.

Quick Order SKU Lookup

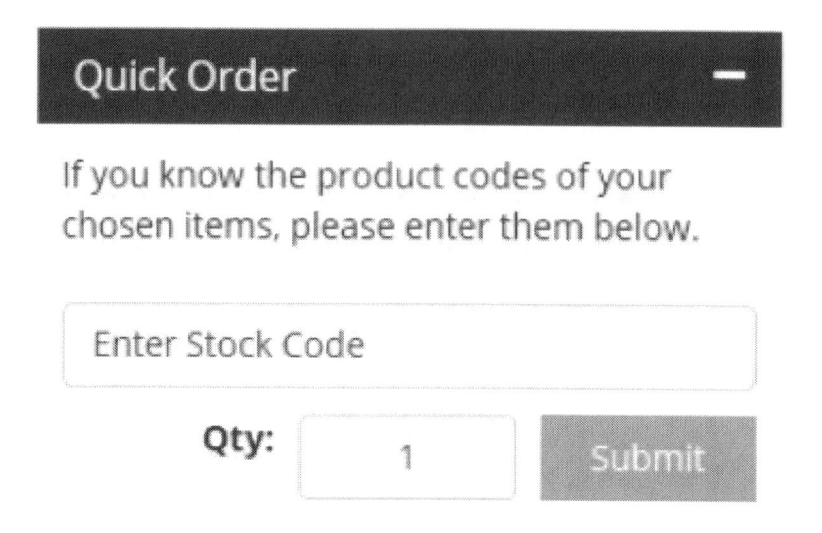

Quick Order

If you know the product codes of your chosen items, please enter them below.

Enter Stock Code

Qty: 1 Submit

This one isn't completely unique to B2B; you'll often find a quick order option on a B2C website if they also mail a catalogue.

It enables a customer who knows their stock/SKU codes to very quickly place an order. Simply put in the code and the quantity, then hit submit.

Definitely one to consider if your B2B customers tend to order only one or two items at a time.

Repeat Past Orders

Discount	£0.00
Total	£218.42
VAT	£43.68
Total (inc VAT)	£262.10

[Repeat Order]

Back to Order History

If your customers frequently place very similar orders, you should consider giving them access to all their past orders on your website, which enables them to tweak that order and place it again. Give them the option to remove products, and change the quantities.

Once they've hit the "Repeat Order" button, they should then be able to either add extra items to the order, or go straight to checkout.

Personal Best Seller List

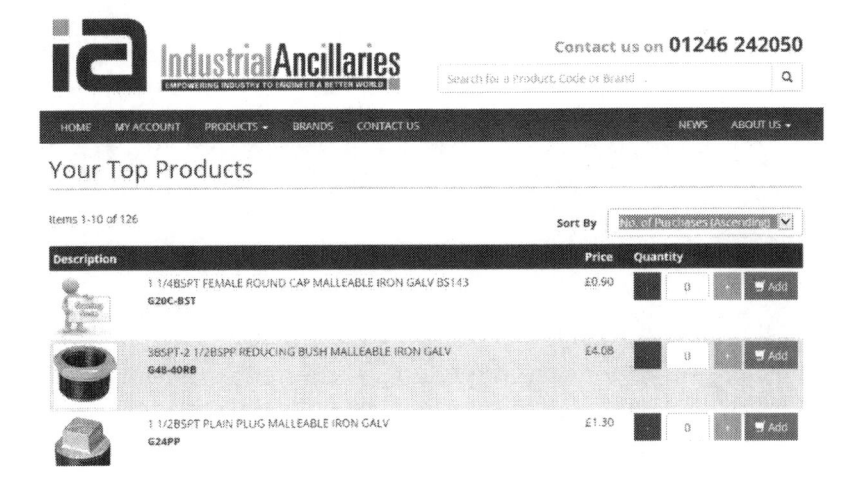

Industrial Ancillaries
EMPOWERING INDUSTRY TO ENGINEER A BETTER WORLD

Contact us on **01246 242050**

Search for a Product, Code or Brand

HOME | MY ACCOUNT | PRODUCTS | BRANDS | CONTACT US | NEWS | ABOUT US

Your Top Products

Items 3-10 of 126   Sort By: No. of Purchases (Ascending)

Description	Price	Quantity
1 1/4BSPT FEMALE ROUND CAP MALLEABLE IRON GALV BS143 G20C-BST	£0.90	0 [Add]
3BSPT-2 1/2BSPP REDUCING BUSH MALLEABLE IRON GALV G48-40RB	£4.08	0 [Add]
1 1/2BSPT PLAIN PLUG MALLEABLE IRON GALV G24PP	£1.30	0 [Add]

A B2C eCommerce site often has a 'Bestsellers' area where a customer can see what the overall best-selling products are. This is a stage better!

If your B2B buyers are buying frequently from you, create for them their own personalised product category that lists the products they, personally, buy most often.

This gives them another quick way to place that order. The easier you make it for them, the happier the customer will be; the happier the customer is, the more they will spend with you.

Current Offers Section

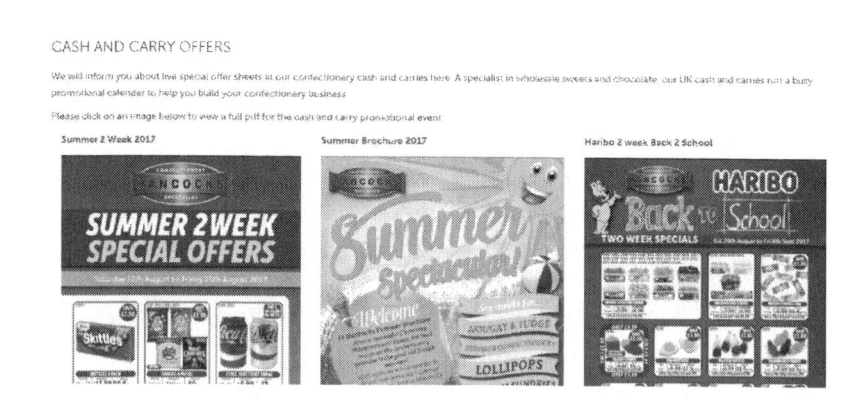

This is a somewhat less complex piece of functionality!

It's a page which summarises the current offers that are available to your customers. In this case, the customer can download a one-page PDF flyer of each current offer set.

A very simple way to keep the customers informed of any deals you have happening.

10 Lessons in Site Building

Throughout my career, I've been involved in website builds and rebuilds. Between 2004 and 2012, I project-managed over 20 eCommerce website builds and redesigns on over 10 different software platforms with budgets ranging from £2,000 to £150,000. Dealing with stakeholders who knew exactly what they wanted and those who didn't; not all the projects went smoothly or ended well.

Since 2012, I've stopped project managing, but I still advise, and assist with builds, and run the occasional tender process. I've learnt a lot, and this chapter is all about helping you learn from my experience.

There are some things that are common across every project I have been involved in, or heard about. Before we go through the process of how to get the website right the first time, I'm going to run through a handful of things it's worth being aware of before you start.

Pretty much of all these are present in even the most perfect site build...

You Will Fall Out

At some point in the project, you will fall out with your website builder.

It might not be a screaming match, but during the build or sign-off phase, there will be a point at which you seriously consider sacking the website builders, and starting again.

I'd say 9 times out of 10, you shouldn't!

Falling out and butting heads is natural in such a big and important project.

It's really complex, you have a massive amount invested in the process, and it's a scary process.

It's a process that will take months, and it's not until the site gets delivered that you find out if it was worth it. Of course, you are going to fall out with them, or be disappointed.

If the whole thing goes smoothly, 100% of the way through, then you have probably not pushed hard enough to get the site you want.

When the Site Finally Goes Live, You'll Want to Hug Your Site Builders

Until a website is finished and live, it's hard to see how it's really going to work because the only true measure is what it does to your sales.

In the last few days of the project, it will suddenly come together and, once the site is live, you'll finally realise the benefits the site has brought you: Sales will go up, the customers will love the ability to order without having to pick up the phone, and the sales team will be claiming it all was all their idea.

At this point, you will be just a little bit in love with your website builder and very, very relieved.

The Last Week Before the Site Goes Live Will Be Crazy

There will be so much to do, so many pages to proof, so much content to upload and check, and endless testing of checkout functionality. You will wonder what you did before the website build project started.

You will underestimate the time required to do all the testing, and a world of little issues will crop up.

Be ready for a lot of diary flexibility. Especially because…

Timescales Will Stretch

And it will be completely outside your control:

- Other projects or crises arise within your own business.
- Something crops up that wasn't in the brief but turns out to be essential and is going to take time to build, integrate and test.
- The website builders underestimated the complexity of the build, or their premises gets flooded.

So, never announce the live date until the day after it happens (or at least when you're 100% sure it's going to happen).

That's why launch and live are two separate things.

Live is when the site goes live and your launch date is when you are happy you're ready to launch the website — to tell the world it exists.

Something Not in the Brief Will Turn Out to Be Critical

This doesn't mean anyone did anything wrong; it's just the way things evolve.

Maybe your site builder has just built a very cool warranty claim system for someone else and you're like "oh, my, god, we have to have that".

Maybe something you're integrating with will change the integration requirements.

Maybe the marketing team has discovered that the customers LOVE 'how to use' videos, and it would be crazy not to put them on the product pages.

These are things worth changing the brief for — and dealing with any time slips.

However Good Your Brief Is, It Will Change

Yes, new things may crop up. You may also need to remove things you wanted — maybe there's a different way to achieve the same outcome that's quicker and cheaper?

Maybe something you wanted just isn't possible.

That's ok, but make sure everyone is aware of, and accepts any changes. And try to keep those that adversely affect time, money, and the eventual customer experience to a minimum.

The biggest changes tend to happen between you sending it to the website builders and when you sign on the dotted line and the project actually kicks off. That's because your website builders will have ideas about how the site in your brief can be improved; things you thought would be out of the price range may not be, and it may be possible to do other things better.

Your Site Will Never Be Finished

Yes, there will be a "woo-hoo, we're live, the project is over" moment — but then the optimisation begins.

You'll be listening to your customers, watching the stats, and working through all those ideas you had during build that you think will improve performance.

The good news is that, given it will never be finished, you don't have to have every single last possible idea live on day one. You can go out there with the MVP (minimum viable product) to test if the customers really do want to buy from you online, then build in more functionality later.

Must Be a Great Site on Day One

Even if you're launching an MVP, it still has to be a great site on day one. That's for two very important reasons

1. You're going to be asking your existing customers to buy from this site, and they're used to a certain standard of information, branding, and service from your business. The website must live up to that, or you're going to disappoint them.

6. People are now very used to buying from eCommerce sites that work — so yours must work.

Bear all these points in mind as we go through the process of building that first website.

11 7 Steps to Get Your Site Built Right First Time

You can download various useful tools for planning and managing a website build from eCommerceMasterPlan.com/freeb2b, including a workbook for this section.

They say buying a house and buying a car are the most stressful experiences of anyone's life. This surely only relates to people who aren't responsible for building an eCommerce website.

Hopefully, I haven't scared you off the idea of building an eCommerce website...

The key to a successful build lies in the planning.

A successful build means:

- You get a website that includes the functionality you need to serve your customers.
- You pay a fair price for that site.
- The site goes live within an acceptable timeframe.
- Ultimately you want it to drive sales, so it should do that well, too.

Problems that get in the way of achieving a successful build are usually caused by:

- In-house stakeholders aren't in agreement, so the scope changes mid-project.
- Brief not detailed enough.
- Assumptions: What you wrote in the brief and what the website builder read in the brief was understood in different ways. You said 'Zoom' and meant bigger-picture-in-a-pop-up; they heard 'Zoom' and thought fully interactive zoom and image rotation.
- (Most annoying of all) your original brief failing to outline the website that would work for your customers.

The majority of the failures are built in at the start of the project. That's great because it means you can build them out of the project by keeping your stakeholders involved, creating a clear brief, running a thorough tender process, and choosing the right site builders.

1. Research
2. Creating the brief
3. Deciding who to send the tender to
4. Running the Tender Process
5. Signing and kicking off
6. The build
7. Putting the new site live

Follow this process to make sure you get it right (or as right as possible) first time.

The last time I ran a site build tendering process this way, including writing the tender document, chatting with the client's team, and being in every meeting, took 32 hours of my time over 9 weeks. That was to get from step 1 through to step 4 — just to find the right person to build, not to actually start building.

I'd suggest this is being as efficient as you can sensibly get for the first 4 steps, so it is not a quick or short process.

Step 1: Research: Consult the Stakeholders

In Stage 2, you consulted the stakeholders to make sure everyone was on board with the eCommerce business model idea.

Now it's time to consult those who will be involved in making it happen to ensure the right website is built. Of course, you picked up ideas whilst working through Stage 2, so make sure to record those and discuss them further during this research step.

There are a lot of areas of input into a website for an eCommerce business. It's important to get them all understood early in the process because it will make the whole project easier to manage AND make sure you get the right site.

As a minimum, this should include:

- **The product team (buyers and merchandising)**: Get them involved so you know what the products are and how you need to sell them. Do the products have different sizing or colours? What information needs to be displayed with each product?

- **Online merchandisers**: What do they need to be able to do with the content management system (CMS)?

- **Sales**: What will make the website a great tool for them and their accounts?

- **Customer services**: Find out what key problems the customers have; how can the new site fix these?

(FAQs, 'how to build it' videos, 'call us/email us' buttons.)

- **IT/warehouse**: Integration. It's critical to get this right, as it can save hours and money. Find out what integration they need, and how best to do it.
- **Finance**: What payment methods are you using/can you use?
- **Marketing**: What feeds and tracking do they need? What is required for search engine optimisation (SEO), for social media? What promotions does the website need to be able to run?
- **Brand**: What should the site look like?
- **The owner.**

In your business, there may be more stakeholders than this, so take half an hour to consider who needs to be involved and why. Then work out the easiest way to do this — a half-day meeting of everyone? An email questionnaire? A coffee with each stakeholder?

If yours is a small organisation, some of these responsibilities may be handled by the same person, so make sure you get input from both the different hats they, or you yourself wear.

This is also the point at which you need to make sure the needs of your customers are going to be met, so you may consult with them in this process too. As a minimum, every stakeholder should be considering the needs of the customer, not just the business.

They should also be considering how your site will stack up against the competition, and the objectives that have been agreed upon for the project.

Make sure you also future-proof the site. It's not just about what you need today; discussions should include what's going to be needed over the next 12–36 months. If you're about to launch a range of personalised items, you need the website to be ready.

Once you have the input of all the stakeholders, you may find conflict between them about what they all want. You will have to resolve these conflicts before putting the site out to tender.

As well as gathering everyone's input for the brief, you also need to work out who's going to be actively involved in the process:

- Who's going to check the brief?
- Who's going to come along to the tender meetings?
- Who's going to be helping provide the information and testing the site during the build phase?

Making those roles clear at the start will make the whole project much easier, so explain to each stakeholder what their involvement from here on in will be. You need to manage their expectations and their involvement — what will you need them to sign off at the end of the project, if anything?

Step 2: Creating the Brief

The brief is the document you are going to send out to the companies who are going to tender for the job of building your website. The brief enables you to make sure everything your company needs is going to be provided.

It is where you pull together EVERYTHING you've done so far — objectives, stakeholder feedback, customer needs, etc.

Make the brief really detailed; if it's less than five pages, it does not contain enough information.

I can't emphasize that enough. The more detail you put in the easier it's going to be for you later on. The most recent project I worked on had an 18-page brief.

Reasons to make it detailed:

- Saves you time when comparing the tender responses; each site builder knows exactly what you want.
- Saves you time and money during the build; avoiding surprises means avoiding additional expense and delay.
- Makes sure everything you and your team need is included.
- The website builders will appreciate it! And if they like you, they'll build you a better site. In my last project, half of the companies we tendered thanked us for the quality of the brief.

You may want to include mock-ups of how it might look, as well as an example set of product data. The more detail you put in, the more effective the tendering process will be, and the smoother the website build project.

As well as all the detailed information, it is worth putting in some background colour for the project: Why do you want the new site? What are your hopes for it? Include those objectives you've outlined.

Commonly a brief will include these key sections:

- Overview of your business.
- Aim: What you're hoping to achieve with the site.
- Who's going to be involved in the build.
  - Your team members and their responsibilities.
  - Any outside agencies? PPC, SEO etc?
- Key functionality you need:
  - The B2B eCommerce site structure you're looking for.
  - What's the pricing and promotional structure you need?
  - Delivery options you want/need and how the pricing works for that.
  - Products — how many? What information do they need? What format are they? (colour options/sizing/etc)
  - Payment methods you want to accept (including Purchase Orders and invoicing).

- Customer accounts — how integrated do you want this? What should customers be able to access on the website.
- Email sign up.
- Catalogue request.
- New account request.
- Live chat and other customer-service tools.

• Navigation and design:
- Mobile responsive? Or mobile-first design?
- Who's responsible for the design? Are your designers going to 'colour in' the wire frames provided by the builder? Or is the site builder going to do all the design, but stick to your brand guidelines? (I suggest the latter)
- Content you want to include — blog pages? Video? Product pages with downloadable CAD files?
- Online catalogue?
- Wire frames of pages, if you're clear on how you want them laid out already.

• Technical stuff (Some of these add clarity to what you would normally put in; others are little extras it's worth getting added in.):
- Do you need white label sites in the future?
- Estimate the traffic you'll get (to enable hosting cost calculations).
- Google Shopping Feed, if you want to use Google Adwords to market the website.

- A product information feed for your customers' websites.
- A postcode lookup tool integration (for postal address entering).
- Google Search Console, including XML Feeds (for SEO).
- Google Tag Manager, if you want to manage your own tagging (marketing stuff).
- 301 redirects (if it's not your first website).
- Full Google Analytics tracking, including search and eCommerce.
- Auto-generating metadata for SEO.[30]
- Include which browser/operating system configurations you want the site to work on.[31]

• Integrations
- Even if included in other parts of the brief, I always create a section which confirms every integration required, including details on the integration criteria.

Integrations are the bane of every eCommerce site build.

Be really clear on what systems you're going to need the site to integrate with.

These might include:

---

30   Guidance on this is available at eCommerceMasterPlan.com/freeb2b
31   There is a list of the current ones to include on the website: eCommerceMasterPlan.com/freeb2b

- Email marketing system
- Pick-and-pack system
- Account management system
- Warehouse and inventory

There are many many more!

Once you are happy with the brief, get key stakeholders to check it over: If you get them to all agree at this point, it makes the rest of the process much more straightforward.

Once the whole company is happy with the brief, it is time to start the tendering process.

The tender process involves:

- Selecting who to send your brief to.
- Managing them so you get the information you need to pick the right provider for you.

Employ too simple a tender process and you risk choosing the wrong company because you don't have enough information.

Too long-winded a tender process and you risk choosing the wrong company because you forget who's who.

The following steps are my tried-and-tested process for getting to the right decision in as short a time span as possible, minimising both the days between start and finish, and the hours you and your team spend on it.

Step 3: Deciding Who to Send The Tender to

It may take a bit of digging to find the right people to finally send your brief out to, so I recommend you start by creating a big long list of potential companies. And then slimming that list down to 3-5 by checking them against your key criteria.

Many of the case studies in this book show just how important it is to find the right company to build your site, so it is definitely worth investing time to find the right options.

Create your Long List

There's lots of ways to find site builders for your long list, including:

- Your existing provider (if you have one); it's only polite to include them.

- Ask anyone important you integrate with (e.g., your order processing software system) who they recommend. Integration with back-end systems is both the biggest risk and the biggest expense, so if they can recommend some businesses who've already done it well, that's a big step forward. (This actually gave us our winner in my most recent project.)

- Ask your customers: Tweet, Facebook, email your customers saying that you're looking for someone to build you a new site. You never know which fantastic eCommerce site builder has been buying from you for a while, just WISHING they could help.

- Putting it out on social media will also help you find companies who are savvy and hungry, as they'll recommend themselves. Great places to do this are LinkedIn and Facebook Groups[32], e.g: "looking for a website builder who has experience building B2B eCommerce sites with complex account-based pricing structures, and huge SKU counts; who would you recommend?"

- Ask your suppliers in the eCommerce fields for recommendations, or to tweet it out on your behalf (I quite often do this for people).

- Ask your eCommerce business owner friends for recommendations.

- Search on Google.

- Look at who your competition use, or other B2B eCommerce sites you admire.

This is probably going to lead you to 10-20 possible site builders.

Create your Short List

Only some of those you identified in the Long List are going to be the right builder for you, and it's usually pretty quick and easy to cut them down to just 3 to 5. You really don't want to take any more than 5 into the tender process; it just makes it far too time-consuming.

---

32 You could ask in my Facebook Group – eCommerce MasterPlan World. Find it via eCommerceMasterPlan.com/facebook

Work out which criteria are the most important to you; you're looking for things that have a Y/N answer. What are the do or die requirements for you?

The key criteria probably include:

- Have you handled {insert type of site build} before? (e.g., B2B with account-based pricing, B2B with spin-off white labelled sites where we'll drop ship for our retail customers, etc.)

- Have you integrated with {insert critical tool here} before? (That might be your accounts system (Sage), or CRM system, or warehouse system.)

- Are you able to cope with {insert critical piece of functionality here}? (e.g., multi-currency, multi-country, PDF downloads on the product pages.)

- What's your usual price range? Many won't want to tell you this, so you may have to have a budget number for them. "Our budget is £x, is that something you would consider?"

- If we wanted it live by X, when would we need to sign on the dotted line? (Just to check they can fit you in!)

- Can you direct me to a couple of similar sites you've built?

Try and get the answers from their website or social media if you can; only call or email them as a last resort. Respect their time, and avoid getting put on their sales list!

Anyone who gets a "no" is off the list. Then go through those who are left, and pick your favourites. Try to get this down to 6 or fewer, but you might want to hold onto a reserve list in case any on the short list don't want the job and decline to send in a proposal.

Sometimes, the answers to those questions remove everyone! In which case, you've either got to go back to the research phase, or decide you're happy to let one or more of your criteria go.

Step 4: Running the Tender Process

Now you have your shortlist it's time to take them through your tendering process.

1. Sending out the tender
2. Manging responses
3. Picking who gets to meet with you
4. Setting up the meetings
5. Meetings week
6. The Final Decision
7. Email the unsuccessful

Templates for each email and document in the tender process are available at eCommerceMasterPlan.com/freeb2b.

Sending out the tender

Send each of those who made it onto the short list a copy of your brief, and also tell them:

- When you expect their response; give them at least 2 weeks, ideally 3.

- Anything you specifically want them to include – e.g., hosting prices, license fees, some references you can call.

- Whether you expect a design treatment with the proposal, or if that will be required for the meeting stage.

- What the next steps will be after this:
  - When you're going to decide who you will be meeting.
  - Details of the meetings – e.g., "we will have a three-hour meeting with each successful tenderer at {location}, hopefully week beginning {date}".
  - When you're aiming to make the final decision.

This last set of information may seem like overkill, but it shows you are serious and gives them an idea of where you'd want to be fitting into their work schedules. That may just help out with pricing and timescales.

I usually include the selection process information in the email as well as in the brief itself.

Hi {name},

{how we found out about you} - we'd like you to consider our project...

Attached is our site scope, including timescales and more.

You need to get your proposal back to us by the 27th March, and it should include:
- costs to do the project
- ongoing costs in hosting etc
- Timescales
- approach
etc

Please liaise with me during this stage of the process.

If you have any questions please EMAIL them to me by 13th March (I'm on holiday w/b 23rd, and will need time to get back to you), and I will make sure you get the answers, and that any relevant answers from other website builders are provided to everyone as well.

Thanks!
Chloe

Whilst waiting on responses

Two key rules during this time:

1. Be fair

   Whilst it's always nice to be fair, it's also important in helping you make the right decision. If you've provided just one of them with five extra pieces of information, and not given that to the rest you won't be comparing apples with apples. Which means you risk making a bad decision.

   - If anyone asks for a meeting, refuse them. It's not fair to the others if one gets a meeting and the rest don't, and it's really time-consuming.

   - They will all come back with questions; send the additional info to everyone. To make this process easier, I tend to batch it, emailing everyone twice a week with ALL answers in one go.

2. Wait until you have all the proposals back before reading any of them.

   - Makes it easier to compare them if you look at all of them with fresh eyes.
   - Saves you time! A lot of time.

Picking who gets to meet with you

Each builder will come back to you in a different way. That's OK. The structure they come back with enables them to fit their technology to your needs in the easiest way for them. You want them to do a good job if you pick them, so making it easy for them to do the job will save you time and money, and reduce errors.

Letting them respond in their own style also gives you an insight into how they work, and that's a great thing to find out, too. If the proposal is disjointed and full of errors and inaccuracies, be very wary!

From each builder, you will expect to get back:

- **Pricing**: Both build cost and future maintenance costs such as hosting fees. Ideally, the cost will be broken down so you can see if you want to exclude anything. Never buy a website based only on the build price. Website pricing is more complicated than that. There will always be follow-on costs such as hosting, software license fees, maintenance, and support retainers. You need to factor in what these are, and fully understand what is and isn't covered in the overall price. Try to extrapolate each builder's fees over 12–24 months to get a proper basis for comparison.

- **Timescales**: These might be exact dates, or simply usual timeframes.
- **References**: A few customers you can speak to.
- **Everything you requested**: Building a new website is a job where nothing can be forgotten or overlooked. So, if they've ignored or forgotten to include something you specifically asked for, that's a black mark in my book.

Fairly evaluate each proposal and see if you can reduce the number of site builders you're going to bring in for a meeting.

Key things to remember:

- No one's been able to meet with you yet, so ignore rough edges on pricing, and minor misunderstandings.
- Be aware that different companies invest different amounts of time in their proposals. Don't penalise someone who's provided everything you asked for against someone who's gone overboard. If they're going overboard on every proposal, then they may never have time to build your website.
- You'll probably want someone else's opinion at this point in time! Get the most important stakeholders to have a read too.

Once you and your colleagues have been through it all, get together and decide who to bring in for a meeting. You need at least 3 possibles to give you a good selection to choose from, and I always aim to bring a mix of different solutions. I always try to bring in a scarily cheap one and a scarily expensive one; one of them might be the only one who actually understood the brief!!

Don't forget to make sure your systems team is happy with the integration plans.

Emailing the unsuccessful

Please please please do email them. To a sales person, a 'no' is as good as a 'yes' sometimes because you get to cross it off the list. Plus, it's only polite!

Emailing the successful & setting up the meetings

Setting up the meetings with those you want to see is where a lot of time can be wasted.

If you spread the meetings over several weeks, it becomes a LOT harder to choose between them. I advocate doing all the meetings back to back, in one week.

You should have flagged when meetings were going to happen in your invitation to tender, so all should be able to meet then.

In the last tender I did, we saw four companies in two days, with 3 hours allotted for each. In Cornwall. Whilst one was a Cornish company, the others each travelled at least 3 hours to get to us. Making it this organised is very possible.

Make sure those at your company who need to be in the meeting have the diary space too.

Then it's time to send those emails.

In the email include:

- The agenda
    - Include key topics you want to cover, including anything that's been added to the mix from reading the tenders.
    - A CMS (content management system) run-through — a live run-through of their back-end system will help you understand how easy the CMS (Content Management System) is to use, and how much functionality it gives you.
    - Design: Do you want them to bring mocked-up artwork of what your site would look like? Or would you like a run-through of the front end to find out how much you can tweak?
    - Anything else you think they might need to prepare for in advance.
- Logistics information:
    - The location
    - Facilities available in the meeting room (flip chart, projector etc)
    - Facilities nearby (coffee shop, where to get lunch, parking; you're not testing them on this, so help them out with your local knowledge).
- Reiterate the last steps of the process: When you need their final proposal, and when you'll be making the decision.

At this point, if it's a rebuild, I usually offer Google Analytics access too, not least because I want hosting costs.

I also usually offer more time slots than there are companies so there is some flexibility in getting everyone booked in. In my last tender process we offered 5 slots over 3 days to book 4 meetings.

> **After the meeting**
>
> We'll need you to provide us with the following information:
>
> - Precise hosting costs / license fees
> - Timescale outline by phase
> - Cost outline by phase
> - Revised proposal where relevant.
>
> Ideally we'd like to see that early w/b 11th May so we can make the decision by the end of the week.
>
> **Your meeting slot**
>
> Meetings will take place at the Tremough Innovation Centre (Tremough Campus, Penryn, Cornwall TR10 9TA).
> Morning session 9.30-12.30
> Afternoon session 1.30-4.30
>
> Days
> Weds 6th am and pm
> Thurs 7th am and pm
> Fri 8th am
>
> It's first come first served, and whilst there are some slots outside this if needs be - we'd really like to get this done during the above... so we can make a quick decision and get things moving.
>
> Any qs in the meantime, please let me know
>
> Cheers
> Chloe

Each meeting you have will prompt fresh questions, so if you can, I'd recommend meeting the 'worst' first and your favourite last so you can ask all those fresh questions of your favourite right there and then.

Meetings week

Clear your diary for the days you are meeting tenderers.

You want to keep your head in the game, and it's going to be a set of intense 3-hour sessions.

Each meeting deserves your full attention. Turn. Off. Your. Phone.

I strongly suggest you prepare for all the meetings before you have the first one. You may find a question prompted by one tender is actually one you want to ask of everyone.

You'll want these on hand during the meetings:

- A printed copy of each tender, with your notes and key questions you want to ask:
  - Question anything that doesn't make sense to you in their response. This is your opportunity to really understand what they can/can't do for you.
  - Ask about timescales: When can they fit in your build? How busy are they right now?
  - How much stretch have the builders allowed for in the project? What happens if the costs and timescales grow beyond this?
- A schedule for the week detailing, who, when: This is literally name, company name, and time! (You don't want to accidentally call Jill Jane!)
- A score sheet for each site builder.

The score sheet you should fill in at the end of each meeting, and each person on your side should fill in the score sheet separately. This makes it really easy to remember who was who, and compare them at the end of the week to make your decision.

This is the score sheet we used; put in the criteria that's critical to your build (probably the same as your points on the agenda)! Don't just copy my list!!

Vendor: _____   Out of 10 before meet: _____

Post meeting scores:	Out of 10
Get the project and us	
Backend	
Integration	
Design	
People	
SEO	
Load speed	
Price	
Timescale	
General feel	
TOTAL	/ 100

At the end of each meeting, confirm what extra information you need back from them and by when. I recommend you give everyone the chance to reprice (either up or down) based on their greater understanding of the project. And ask for both build cost and ongoing costs — licenses, fees, subscriptions, hosting, as well as timescales.

Once each meeting is over, and before your team leaves the room or gets distracted by email, make sure they fill out their score sheet for the meeting you've just had and have a quick debrief.

The meetings week will be a rollercoaster. Everyone you meet will most likely be capable of doing a good job of your site. Try and get excited about everyone. Your job is to work out who you want to work with for the next three years.

Drop each of the tenderers an email to confirm:

- Any extra information you need.
- When you need it by.
- When you'll be making your choice.

> Hi [name],
>
> Thanks for coming along to our meeting, it was really good to meet you and discuss the project in person. I hope you had a safe journey back.
>
> Triggered by other tender meetings I've a handful of questions it would be great if you could come back to me on, we don't need war and peace - just a quick answer will suffice!
>
> - {add as necessary}
>
> Please get those answers, and confirmation of your proposal (if anything has changed due to the meeting or the above) to us by end of play Monday __th.
>
> I don't anticipate there being anything else we'll ask for.
>
> Once we have everyone's final information we aim to make a decision by Friday at the absolute latest.
>
> Cheers
> Chloe

I recommend doing this after all the meetings have happened, as it gives you the chance to check anything that's emerged during subsequent meetings — e.g., live chat wasn't in scope until the last tenderer convinced you it should be. So you now need to know if everyone else can incorporate that and whether it does anything to their costs or timescales.

The Final Decision

Once you have had the meeting and any final information has come in, you need to pick your favourite. The score sheets and opinions of your team should help make this a quick decision.

Before you let them know the good news, you need to speak to people they have already built sites for and road-test their websites. Key questions to ask previous clients are:

- Was the project on time?
- Was the project on budget?
- How were they to work with?
- How have the support and costs been since the site went live?

The last question is possibly the most important. If the site build goes well, you could be working with the company for years. You need to understand what they are like to work with post-live.

Assuming you are happy with the answers you get, then well done — you've found your site builder!

If you're not happy with the answers, then move on to your second choice and again go out to their clients to check whether your choice is a good one.

Once you're happy you've found the right website builder for you, give them the good news.

Email the unsuccessful

Tell those who haven't been chosen this time.

They will probably request feedback, so be ready to provide a few bullet points about why you made your decision.

Step 5: Signing and Kicking off

Once you've told them that they're the winner, you are going to need to sign some sort of contract with them.

This is a great opportunity to finalise exactly what's in the brief. It won't be the same one that you sent to them in the beginning; you'll have learnt things you want to include during the tender process, and they will have pulled the brief into their format. So, before you sign, take time to make sure you are 100% agreed on the final scope, pricing, payment plan, and timescales.

Step 6: The Build

Now the fun part begins: You have done everything possible to make sure you've picked the right website builder to partner with, and that they are ready to build your prefect B2B eCommerce website. So now it's time to make it a reality.

You quickly need to get clarity on the detail in the timescales/project plan and what you need to do to make it a success.

Most website builders will tell you they have a project manager who will oversee everything for you. I have never worked with one who successfully does. I have worked with many great website-builder-side project managers, but, however good they are, they are not a member of your team; they are a member of the website builder's team. They don't understand what you are trying to achieve as well as you do, and they are highly unlikely to invest time motivating your team to provide things on time and correctly. So, you need to manage the project, too.

As soon as you are under way, convert the brief/to-do-list into whatever format you need it to be in to make sure everything happens and happens right.

The format should be what works for you, be that a mind map, a project planning tool (Asana, Trello, Slack), an Excel spreadsheet, a Google doc, or a very large whiteboard. Get everything on it and explain to the key people how it's to be used (especially the website-builder-side project manager). If you do it really successfully, it will become your key method of communication with the website builders — the foundation of every call and meeting agenda.

Its role is to make sure you always have the answers to these questions:

- What do we need to supply?
- When is everything required?
- When are members of your team going to need to be ready to sign off?
- And how much movement is there in the plan?

Put all the important dates in your diary — and in the diary of anyone else who needs to contribute.

Keep referring back to the agreed scope. Try not to go beyond it and, if the builders are not following it, bring them back on track as soon as possible.

There's a list of possible tools you could use for this, and an example website project planner available from: eCommerceMasterPlan.com/freeb2b.

Step 7: Putting the New Site Live

The first rule of putting the new website live is to make sure you are 100% happy with it. Test everything again and again and again.

For most website builders, the point when the website goes live marks the end of the build phase, so usually any changes after that are chargeable.

It is always tempting to go live with a few things outstanding in order to hit the deadline, but be very careful if you do, because you might be stuck with a very large bill.

A few days before the site goes live, make sure you have access to the DNS hosting for your domain (www.your-website.com). Then change the TTL to a few minutes or seconds; the TTL is the Time to Live — that is how often your domain records are refreshed so, if it's set to 24 hours, it will take a long time for your new website to go live.

Once you're ready to go live:

- Turn off all your marketing activity that drives traffic to the site you're putting live (if this is your first site, don't worry about this!).
- Tell customer services.

- At the appointed time, change the A record of your domain/URL to point to the new hosting IP address.

The A record is the DNS record associated with a URL (aka domain) that tells the internet where to send anyone looking for that website. So when someone types in your website URL (e.g. yourwebsite.com) it makes sure they get to the right IP address (the unique location of the server your website is stored on). It's the simplest and most robust way to do this, and changing the A record is the easiest way to put a new site live.

Whatever you do, do NOT change your domain's Nameservers because doing that delegates total control of your domain to someone else (in this case your website builder). That's bad for two reasons firstly you should always have control of your domain. Secondly, when a nameserver is changed the DNS records you already have in place on that domain aren't taken to the new nameservers. That means your company email (if it uses the same domain eg me@yourwebsite.com) will go down, and so will anything else you are using that domain for.

Once you have changed the A record, there are a few things you need to do almost immediately.

The first is to check that the site is working. Place a few orders, do some navigating, sign up for emails, etc. Make sure it's all working on the front end, but also that any data submitted is ending up where it should (orders to the warehouse, email sign-ups to your database, etc.).

Once you are happy, let the rest of the business know it's changed over.

Be ready to deal with 'but I can still see the old site', and have IT refresh the office cache and individuals' PC caches. It is probably best to explain to everyone that DNS propagation can take a while as all the nameservers around the internet are updated with your new hosting location. This can take a couple of days. An annoying headache, but it is always either the most PC-incompetent person in the office or the boss whose computer is the last to see the new website.

Next, you need to check and set up the non-critical functionality of the new website (that's the stuff that the customers won't have noticed). Is all your tracking code working — analytics and reporting, etc? At this point, you also want to make sure any Google Shopping feeds, Webmaster Tools, etc., are working.

Once all this is done, the site is ready to be marketed!

Before You Move onto Stage 4

Jot down your thoughts.

Answer this question:

- Is your B2B eCommerce site ready to meet your customers?

    Yes   No

If No, get it right before your launch; maybe have a read of the bonus Chapter 17 on what successful websites need.

If Yes, let's get the launch happening! It's time to get working on Stage 4.

Notes

12 Case Study: Gloveman VIP

'It's a tool, not a be-all, end-all replacement'

www.glovemanvip.co.uk

B2B eCommerce MasterPlan | 169

GSL IS A manufacturer and supplier of gloves and consumables to the healthcare industry and beyond, with a turnover of £6.5m. They've been operating for more than 12 years, and started their B2B eCommerce journey in 2012.

They are a 'traditional' (if we can call it that!) business consumables supply company and the core sales team is a call centre of 14, rather than a road-based sales team.

Going eCommerce

In recent years, Gloveman launched both B2C and B2B eCommerce sites on separate platforms (the B2C on EKM Powershop, and the B2B now built by Aspidistra).

They launched the B2C site in order to serve the customer who was happy to pay retail prices, and didn't qualify for a B2B account. So, launching a B2C site has increased sales, and let them tap into a high-margin sector whilst capitalising on the systems they already have set up — customer service, warehouse etc.

The B2B site — "Gloveman VIP" — was initially launched to offer customers something they couldn't get from the competition; to gain a competitive advantage. Unfortunately, the initial launch just didn't work because the first web design agency couldn't get the integration into Sage working properly.

Hence their move to Aspidistra. Since this second site has gone live, they're finally starting to realise the benefits of eCommerce for serving their B2B customers.

Why the Integration With Sage Was the Number One Critical Success Factor

Gloveman's 3,000 customers each have their own negotiated price list, and approved 30-day credit limits.

Credit card payment is possible on the website; customers can pay for their order as they place it, or settle invoices via the website. However, the majority of Gloveman's customers use the website to place orders that they settle once the invoice is raised.

That means it's essential that the website has access to the same account information that the call centre operative has:

- What's the customer's credit limit? Do they have any credit left, or do they need to pay some invoices before they can order more?
- When do those invoices go out?
- If an invoice is overdue by 45 days, don't let them order anything else.
- The correct price list per customer.
- Any delivery charge agreements for that customer.

If this integration isn't fool proof, then it simply makes the website full of loopholes and the potential creator of huge risks.

It also means that, if the customer is on credit-stop, an order can be placed, but won't be shipped until older invoices are cleared. So, Gloveman still gets the order, and it doesn't go to the competition.

Website as Account Management Hub

Now that the Sage integration is fool proof, it's made a host of extra functionality possible on the website so that the customer is in total control of their account.

As well as being able to place orders via the website (by spreadsheet upload as well as by the normal eCommerce "add to basket" method), each customer can access their full account history (all time, not just that placed via the website).

- They can see the status of all invoices, and pay them.
- They can see how much credit they have remaining.
- They can see their previous orders, and use them to create new orders.

Whilst some B2B businesses keep their biggest customers off the website, for Gloveman the biggest customers are the ones who get the most from the eCommerce experience because of the account management hub.

For example, a care agency with their head office in London, but 80 offices around the UK, can have the site set up so that the offices can place their orders, but those orders don't get processed until Head Office signs them off (cancels or amends them). With the whole process managed by the Gloveman VIP site, and with both the Head Office and each office having full view of the status of each order, it all makes things much easier for the B2B customer's team.

A Unique Site for Each B2B Customer

Above we've seen how the account management hub can be customised to better serve the customer, but customisation of a B2B site doesn't stop there.

A few key pieces of day-to-day functionality mean that the whole Gloveman VIP website can be pretty much unique to each customer:

- Each customer has their own product price list (yes, one price list per customer).

- Customers can have access to products no one else has (E.g., products that aren't kept in stock and have slower delivery speeds).

- Each customer can have a unique product selection to order from.

- Customers can have their own delivery price structure (normally it's based on postcode and spend over £x gets it free. But if a customer has negotiated a different rate, that can be set in the website too).

So, each B2B customer can have a completely personalised website experience.

The Challenge of Migration

For the last two years the website has been live and the message to customers has been: 'It's there if you want it'. Gloveman hasn't been actively encouraging customers to switch. During this time, 20% of their customers have converted to using the website.

Increasing that number is something the whole team is now actively engaged in, because the efficiency savings to the business are so great.

These are some of the tactics they're using to increase the uptake:

- **A carrot for the team**: Incentivising the sales team to migrate customers; alongside sales, it's part of their key daily targets.

- **A stick for the customers**: Announcing that statements will no longer be sent by post (invoices will still be posted). Customers must now provide an email address to which statements can be sent, and are encouraged to use the website's account management hub to manage their account status.

- **A carrot for the customers:** Actively educating the customers about the benefits, and talking them through the process. E.g., for the customer who still faxes in a printout of their spreadsheet order, guiding them through how to submit it online, and explaining the benefits (it automatically checks everything, confirms it's in-stock/delivery timings/price, and you'll get the goods quicker).

Overall for Gloveman, the website is there to add value to their company and their products.

It's a tool that's not a replacement for a sales team. Gloveman do not anticipate cutting their sales team even if every single customer migrates to the online offering.

STAGE FOUR

Making B2B eCommerce a Success – Site Launch and Ongoing Marketing

IT IS ONE thing to have a B2B eCommerce site. It's quite another to get customers using it.

In this Stage, we'll run through how to turn your B2B eCommerce website into a successful, contributing part of your business. Contributing because a good B2B eCommerce site will have a positive impact on the whole of your business, not just the eCommerce channel.

13 Launch Is not Live

It's essential to understand this:

Launch ≠ Live

The **Live Date** is the day your website finally goes live. All the building is done, all the products have been populated, all the pricing structures have been tested. It works, it's fully integrated, it is live.

The **Launch Date** is when you introduce your site to the world — when you start telling customers it exists, when you start trying to get traffic to it and orders placed on it.

Of course, you can do them on the same day if you want. But even if this is a relaunch of an existing site, I would still advise you to hold off on the big announcement until a few customers have placed orders and you know all is well.

Good reasons NOT have the same launch and live dates:

- Live is a movable feast: It is very rare that a website goes live on the right day, and having to keep moving all your launch plans is a nightmare.

- Getting it live is a big project: Get it done and out the way before you start the launch.

- Launching the site is a big project: You need to be able to focus on that, and that alone.

- There's going to be quite a bit of post-live testing to do: You want to make sure that's all good before you send lots of customers to the site.

- Given the site is going to be an integral part of the business, you want to make sure the whole business understands what it is and how it works so they can help customers and spread the word too. So, you probably want to run some sessions for the call centre and sales team on the live site before you invite the customers in.

- You may want to have a couple of select customers try it out and give you feedback before you roll it out to everyone.

Putting launch and live on different dates will give you some breathing space, enabling you to do a better launch, and giving you time to ensure the website is completely ready.

Usually the gap between Live and Launch will only be a few days, a week at the most.

So, this means you cannot completely ignore launch until the site is live. Rather, you'll plan the launch whilst you're building the site, but not execute it until you're 100% happy that everything is ready to go.

What Is Launch?

Launch is the campaign of activity you do to announce your website to the world.

You must have a launch because without it, no one will know about the new site you've spent so much time building.

It may start the day after the website went live, or it may start several months after it's gone live.

It may last several months, or it might last a couple of days.

It may cost £1,000s or it might cost nothing.

There is no right or wrong launch, so long as it achieves what you want to achieve. That means there's no 'launch template' I can give you. However, later in this section, I will run you through some ideas and a 6-step process for creating and executing your launch.

Launch Is Only the Beginning

Just like it's crazy to put the website live and then not do a launch to tell people about it, it's crazy to run a launch and then not do any marketing once the launch is over.

So, the launch is just the beginning of the process of getting customers (old and new) to buy from you via the website.

Just like your call centre has to phone out to get some of the orders, just like your sales team has to hit the road to get those sales, just like you have to mail your catalogue to customers, you have to keep marketing your website.

14 Lessons in Marketing

THESE LESSONS IN marketing are a quick set of rules, revelations, and ideas to fast-track your knowledge before we dive into how to plan your launch.

B2B and B2C eCommerce Marketing Are the Same

I often get asked: "How is B2B eCommerce marketing different to B2C eCommerce marketing?".

The answer is that is isn't different.

The way to approach working out which marketing methods to use, and what messages to send, is exactly the same. That process is the key to creating the marketing plan.

You must focus on your customer:

- What marketing methods will work to bring them to the site and get them to buy?
- What messages do they need to hear from us to get them to buy?

There are hundreds of possible answers to those questions, which is why every business needs its own unique marketing plan.

That's where the differences come in— which marketing methods and messages you chose to use to persuade your customers to buy. BUT there isn't one set exclusively for B2B and another for B2C; some of what you chose to do would also work for some B2C businesses, some won't.

The mix that works for you will be unique to your business. Yes, there'll be lots of overlap with other businesses, but the exact mix will be unique to you.

Where B2B does get different from B2C is in the implementation. For example:

- Pretty much no B2C eCommerce business phones their customers to ask them to order.
- You may find LinkedIn a better social network and advertising channel than Facebook.
- Your events are industry trade shows; their events are pop-up stores or craft fairs.

Segmentation

I find people often either ignore segmentation completely, or get completely obsessed with how they can segment and forget to consider why they might want to segment.

Both are equally bad.

Segmentation means putting a different message in front of a different group of people. You can segment in so many different ways (gender, actions, geography) and on so many different platforms (email, direct mail, online advertising) it can all get rather overwhelming.

If you're considering segmenting, then find the problem/opportunity before you start getting excited about the solution. Let me explain.

- **Problem/Opportunity First**: If you have lots of customers on your database who haven't placed an order in the last six months, and usually your customers order every week, then you have an opportunity. Split these people out (segment them) and send them a series of marketing communications to encourage them to buy again. A great idea.

- **Solution First**: We can segment our customers based on where they are in the country — let's send them an email with a picture of their county. Why?!

Common segmentations you may want to consider in B2B marketing include what sort of customer they are and what the role of each person is within the buying organisation.

What sort of customer are they?

This might focus on which of your products they buy. Is it the high-end range or the basic products? Is it the sweets or the biscuits?

The size of their account, how much do they spend with you each year?

Their industry sector.

What level of relationship do they have with your business? Are they a company that buys every week? Or have never bought at all? Or someone who used to buy every week, and hasn't ordered in the last month?

What the person's role is in the buyer organisation?

Often your business will deal with multiple people at each of your B2B buyer organisations: Accounts to get things paid, the head office buying team to get orders signed off, each brand manager who actually places the order.

Some sales and marketing communications should go to all of them, but others only to certain people.

Your sales team isn't going to visit every single branch and negotiate prices that way; they'll liaise with the head office buying team.

There's little point in telling accounts that this week you have an offer on widget A.

Chloë's Promotional Golden Rule

"A promotion exists to get the customer to do what you want them to do as cheaply as possible."

That goes for any promotion ever — an email, a visit, a catalogue, and the offer or call to action you're using.

The cost is, of course, measured in time, money, and the opportunity cost.

It will be very tempting to include some financial incentive (either to the sales team or the customer) to get those orders coming in through the website. I advise against that during the launch so you're not wasting money converting those who are ready to just use it because they see the inherent benefits. Save the budget for converting those who need the extra convincing.

Do not just throw money at it.

Other Promotional Tips

In addition to bearing in mind my Golden Rule for Promotions, here are some more tips for making sure you get the right result from your promotional activity.

Each of these is a tried-and-tested way to improve response that seems to work in any market, via any channel, and with any product.

Think of these as bankers to bring a great result.

Clear Calls to Action

It seems obvious, but we all need to be reminded of this one from time to time.

Never be afraid to tell your customer what you want them to do.

In every communication, make it really clear what it is you want them to do — that's the call to action.

It might be as simple as saying "please visit the website and sign up", "Click here", "Buy Now", or you might need to weave it into your copy, or show the step-by-step of how to do something.

Always have a clear Call To Action.

Social proof

CUSTOMER TESTIMONIALS

Proudly presenting you with a selection of the praise that we have directly received from our customers recently:

The branch [of Hancocks] I would like to provide feedback on is the Newcastle branch which is based in Drum Lane industrial estate near to Chester Le Street.

I would like to pass on my thanks to the team there. I have been trading for a year now and could not have done this without the help of the managers Tony and Dave and their team. Not only are they knowledgeable about the products they supply but they are always pleasant and approachable. If I have a query (which is quite often) they will always help. The managers always point out their special offers to me and the warehouse is always stocked.

I sell American candy in the shop and the products they supply have increased and are varied. Again this has helped my business to expand. Could you please pass on my thanks and appreciation to the team.

Kind regards

Barbara Ohagan
Bon Bons

This is my absolute favourite.

Social proof is anything that shows the customer that other people trust your business or love that product. For example:

- A customer testimonial.

- A product review.
- How many review stars a product has.
- How many review stars your business has.
- How many reviews your business/that product has.
- Press write ups.
- Number of customers.
- Biggest in the market.
- Famous customers.

Putting out all/any of these will increase your sales and the response to any marketing activity.

Krossover added a testimonial and review score to their remarketing ads (selling game analysis software to football coaches) and increased click-through rate by 45%[33].

---

33   Krossover's reviews boost retargeting CTR by 45%, June 2017 (Trustpilot):
    blog.trustpilot.com/blog/2016/3/21/krossovers-reviews-boost-retargeting-ctr-by-45

It works on everything, because we humans are programmed to feel safer doing things other people have already done, and even more safe if the other people liked it.

Show your customers that you are a safe pair of hands with social proof.

Scarcity

This is where you tell the customer that there's only one/ten/a handful remaining. It gets them to buy faster, because they don't want to miss out.

Deadlines

⊙ Next day delivery for pre-5pm orders   **0 5 3** for **Same Day** Despatch *
                                          Days Hrs Mins

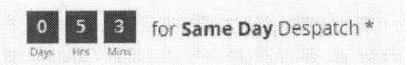

This again plays on the fear of missing out — they have to act by a certain time and date to get the deal/product/etc.

The shorter the deadline, the bigger the response, usually.

Free delivery

🚚 Free delivery on orders over £195

The most powerful driver of online sales. Works better than 10% off, 20% off etc.

Sales or Marketing?

In B2B eCommerce, the line between what is sales and what is marketing gets very blurred.

Your marketing methods (email, social media etc) should drive sales and attract new customers, jobs traditionally done by the sales team.

Your sales methods (sales team, call centre) should be putting forward the same messages and CTAs as in your marketing.

So rather than think of them in silos, just consider what needs to happen to hit your objectives.

The Site Is a New Order-Taking Channel, Being Online Opens Up Lots of New Ways to Drive Sales

That gives you new marketing methods to use, but don't forget the old ones! Your launch activity should embrace both old and new marketing methods.

You can't ignore the real world. A great salesperson and attendance at trade shows will make a huge difference in most markets.

Think of marketing methods as ways to get the message to the customer. So that includes:

- The sales team
- The call centre team
- The accounts team
- Existing and new postal mailings:
    - Invoices
    - Parcels
    - Catalogues
    - Postcards
- Events and conferences
- Email marketing
- Advertising:
    - In trade magazines
    - On trade websites
    - Across the PPC platforms like Google and Facebook
- PR to both online and offline publications

Which of these become part of the launch is up to you, but the website should now be part of every marketing activity you undertake.

Onboarding Will Be Key

Need Help?
01209 314759
info@gloveman.co.uk

Helping your customers through placing their first order on the site is going to be key to keeping them using it.

Your communications about the new site should guide them through the process and offer assistance to help them use it.

Your sales and call centre team should be ready to walk each customer through the process.

There are some great tools you can use so you can see exactly what they're doing on screen; my current favourite is zoom.us.

Retention Is Critical

This one is a huge difference between B2B and B2C eCommerce businesses.

- 90% of a B2C marketer's job is finding new customers.
- 90% of a B2B marketer's job is keeping the existing customers happy and buying.

In B2B, retention is most impacted by customer service.

If you can be a reliable supplier who's there when they need you and able to help with their problem, then they'll keep buying from you.

So, your customer support team (anyone who directly interacts with customers) needs to be fully ready for launch.

Your warehouse team, your call centre, the sales team, and suppliers like your couriers must all be ready for launch.

Your site must be working great for launch.

The stakes are high, so make sure everything is in place to make sure ordering online increases your customer's satisfaction and doesn't send them looking for new suppliers.

Social Media: How Personal Should It Be?

This one really does depend on your customer type.

Often in B2B, social media is most powerful in enhancing the personal relationships between your customers and your key team members — those who regularly interact with customer in the 'real' world — rather than enhancing the relationship between brand and customer.

So, once you've worked out which social media channels your customers want to communicate with you on, work out **who** should be communicating with them:

- The brand

- The owner
- Each sales person

And what messages they should be sharing.

Oh, and think Twitter and LinkedIn, not Facebook and Snapchat.

Marketing to the End Customer

This is a whole other ballgame, so approach with care!

If you design and manufacture your own brand of products, you may want to invest in marketing them to the end consumer to help your B2B customer sell more.

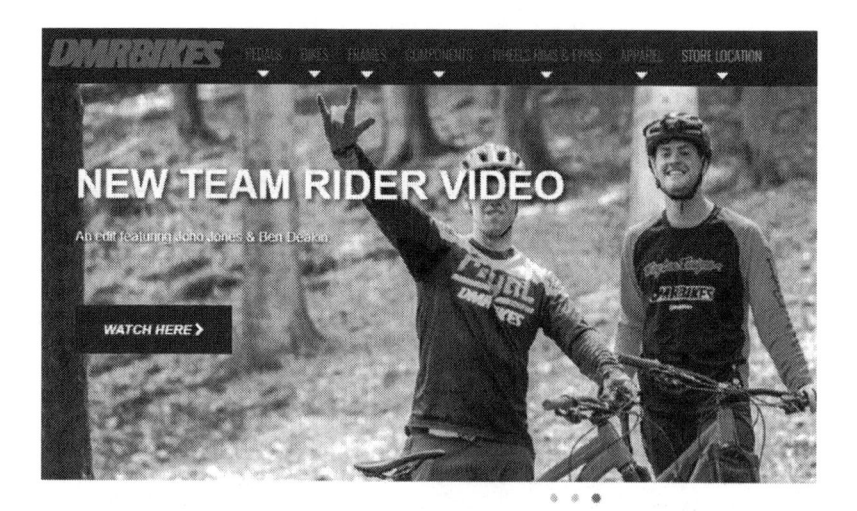

Upgrade Bikes[34] has found this to be a very powerful strategy. Not only has it increased sales of its own brands, it also turned them into the go-to distributor for other companies wanting to wholesale products to the same market. They now distribute and market over 20 brands.

---

34   Find the full Upgrade Bikes case study in Chapter 3.

15 6 Steps to Plan and Execute Your Launch

IN THE LAST two chapters, I've given you lots of ideas about how launches work and things you need to consider in your marketing activity. Now let's get into the nitty gritty of what yours is going to look like.

I've written what follows for launching a B2B eCommerce site for the first time. If you're currently relaunching, or launching new functionality, this method will work for you too, but you may want to simplify if need be.

1. **OBJECTIVES**
   What do you want your launch to achieve?

2. **BUDGET**
   How much can you afford to spend?

3. **MESSAGE**
   What do you want to say to your customers?

4. **MARKETING METHODS**
   How will you get the message out there?

5. **PLAN**
   What are you going to do?

6. **EXECUTE**
   Time to make the plan work

Step 1: Objectives – What Do You Want Your Launch to Achieve?

Before you can start deciding what marketing you're going to do, how much you're going to spend, what you're going to say, you've got to establish what the point of the launch is.

Why are you going to do a launch?

"To tell customers about the new website" is not a good answer!

You need to consider:

Who

Who do you want to know about the site?

Do you want to tell all your customers? Do you only want to tell the smallest 10%? Or everyone except customers A, B, and C? Is it only customers in the UK? Or only customers overseas? Or only customers who buy a certain product type? Or is it about new customer acquisition?

For launch, you might choose to only target one group of customers, despite the fact that eventually you want to get all customers on there. Maybe you've only added one product category so far, so the customers of that category are the ones that will get this launch (and you'll do another launch as the other product categories are ready).

Phasing a launch like this can be a great way to maximise overall success. Not least because it reduces the workload for the customer services team, as only one group of customers are being onboarded at a time.

Phasing means running a series of mini-launches until the whole customer base is targeted, and all the functionality is live. So maybe your first phase is a launch to Customer Group 1 that lasts for two weeks. Assuming all goes well, you go straight into phase two and launch out to Customer Group 2 over the next two weeks — and so forth.

What

The customers who you've identified — what do you want them to do?

Place their next order on the website? Start managing their invoices online? Never call the office again? Stop requesting a catalogue?

The numbers

The chances are you're not going to get all of them to comply immediately. So, let's put some numbers around the launch objective:

- **Timescale**: How quickly do you want them to do it?
- **Volume**: How many of them do you want to do it?

Putting all that together will give you your Launch Objective:

"To get 50% of our top 100 customers to place an order via the website in the next 90 days."

More than one objective

Your launch may have more than one objective, e.g:

Objective A:
"To get 50% of our top 100 customers to place an order via the website in the next 90 days."

Objective B:
"To migrate all our customers with credit limits under £10k from paper invoices to the online account system in the next 30 days."

If you chose to run a phased launch program – maybe 20% of your customers at a time, or one product category at a time — set an overall objective, and another for each launch phase.

The reason you need an objective is that it gives clarity to you and your team about what the business wants to achieve with the launch.

Step 2: Budget – How Much Can You Afford to Spend?

You shouldn't do anything in business (or life?) without a clear budget.

Of course, you could choose to work that out after you've decided what marketing you want to do and just add up how much that will cost.

Probably better though to work out how much achieving each objective is worth to the business, then set that as your budget. If you are planning multiple phases or objectives, set one budget for each.

Once you know the budget, you can then work out how best to spend it to hit the objectives.

Step 3: Message – What Do You Want to Say to Your Customers?

"Please use our new website" (probably) isn't going to cut it.

What is the message you want to get across to the selected customers? It's going to be used in your marketing, on the website itself, and as your team interacts with your customers. So it's super-important that everyone is clear on exactly what the key message is[35].

If the objective is to get them to place their first order online, then the message should focus on the benefits to them — faster service, instant stock confirmation, order 24/7.

If the objective is to get them to manage their account online, then, as well as the benefits, you're probably going to need to include some pain points — all your invoices, ever, in one place; as of 31st May we will no longer be posting invoices.

If there are negative messages, then it would be worth briefing your team on how to deal with kickback from customers about these. How to explain the benefits of invoices no longer coming through the post, and how to make it clear there will be no exceptions.

Don't forget those promotional tips we ran through above; you may want to use them to construct a strong CTA. For example:

- To celebrate the launch of our new eCommerce site, we're offering free delivery to everyone who registers

---

35 Walcot House has a great justification of why they've gone eCommerce on their website:
    walcothouse.com/pages/a-word-from-the-boss

and places their first order by Friday. [Deadline + Free delivery]

- The first 100 customers to register will get free delivery on all orders placed via the website for the next month. [Scarcity + Free delivery]

- Book your onboarding session with one of our team – we can only fit in 10 per day – so book now to make sure it fits with your schedules. [Scarcity]

And in every email/advertisement, I'd have a customer quote about how easy they found the website to use.

Step 4: Marketing Methods – How Will You Get the Message Out There?

Just how are you going to let the customers know about the new website?

How many marketing methods you use in your launch will depend on how many you need to use to make sure your objectives are achieved.

Which methods you use will depend on what you already have in place, how your customers expect to be communicated with, and what works best in your sector.

You may decide the launch is a good time to test new communication methods too.

You may decide that you'll definitely use some channels, and roll the launch out to some others if it's not going as well as you hoped. We'll use email and phone, and if we need to, we'll send some direct mail.

You may also decide to use some methods for some customers, but not for others. You may let your biggest customers know and explain the new system in a face-to-face meeting, but tell the smaller customers by email.

There are no right or wrong choices for your launch; it's about working out what marketing methods will best help you achieve your objectives.

Here's some ideas for you.

Likely channels for getting the message to existing customers

First and foremost, you want to utilise the channels you already use to communicate with your customers. That might include:

- The sales team and ordering channels
  - On the phone
  - Personal emails
  - Phone calls
  - Faxes!
- Email marketing / mass email sends
- SMS (text messaging)

- Direct mail — on the cover of the catalogue or an insert or postcard
- At an event or conference
- Social media
- PR

Next there are the new channels that maybe you haven't used to communicate with your customers:

- **Email marketing**: This is the big one, the one that usually hasn't been used, but has huge potential to produce results. It's one that's going to be important to drive sales to your new website post-launch, so I highly recommend making sure email marketing is part of your launch plan.

- **SMS**: If your customers are not usually tied to their desks, you may find sending the message out so it reaches their mobile device works well for you. If you're going to do this, I suggest you send a text saying, "Find out how our new website is going to help you out" with a link to a page that explains the benefits and how it works, NOT sending a message "we've got a new website" that takes them to the homepage.

- **Social media**: Similar to SMS really, although this one will also pick up those who aren't yet your customers.

- **Direct Mail**: If you've never communicated via direct mail, I highly recommend sending something by post for your launch. DM can have a huge impact on results. Just a simple letter or postcard, or you could get creative and send a mouse mat or mug with the new website address on it.

- **PR**: Get an article in your key industry press titles; this will of course get the message in front of potential customers too.

- **Webinars**: You may want to run a series of online webinars (like a presentation, but delivered online) that your customers can join in on to find out all about the new site and services. Structure it with a presentation to take them through the key benefits and how it works, give them clear next steps to take, and have an open Q&A session, too.

Likely channels for getting the message to new customers

If one of your launch objectives is to get the message out to new customers, then that opens up some more opportunities.

Of course, for new customers, the message is probably going to be different. Rather than explaining how things are going to be different, it might be enough to say, "you can now order online", or simply let them know you exist.

Here are some ideas for how you might like to get the message in front of potential new customers:

- **The sales team**: If you have a list of prospects who you haven't yet converted to customers, the ease of online ordering might just tip them over to you.

- **Email marketing**: If you have a list of prospects who have enquired but never become customers, sending them emails about your new service would be a good idea.

- **Advertising (online and offline):** Just like you might use PR and events to let your existing customers know, you could use advertising to get to the existing customers. But I wouldn't until the other avenues have been exhausted. I'd save advertising for getting new customers on board. There are lots of different advertising methods you could employ; each requires different budget levels, and will bring different results. Here's some ideas:
  - **Industry press:** On and offline
  - **Online display advertising:** Via Google
  - **Advertising:** Use Facebook
  - **Search Engine Advertising:** Via Google and / or Bing. Bidding on keywords related to your products. Maybe even going as far as Google Shopping campaigns [36]

Step 5: Plan – What Are You Going to Do?

Once you've identified the message and the channels (and checked you've got the budget to do it all!), it's time to put that all together into a plan of execution.

Every plan is made to be tweaked, but if you don't have the plan, then you're lost from day one. One of the tricky

---

36   If you'd like to understand more about the various marketing methods you could use, get yourself a copy of my book "eCommerce Marketing: How to Drive Traffic That BUYS to Your Website." Find out all about how to get hold of a copy here: eCommerceMasterPlan.com/books

things with a launch plan is that you must create it before the site goes live, but you won't know when launch is actually happening until live has happened! So, work to your best guess of timings until you have that final live date, then finalise the dates in your plan.

Your plan should be in three formats to make it easy to execute the activity, monitor the activity and make sure everyone involved knows what is happening. The three formats are:

- A calendar of promotional activity – what you're going to do and when
- A written guide to the plan – explaining the research, objectives and thoughts behind the plan
- A target tracking dashboard – to keep you on top of how well the launch is going

A calendar of promotional activity

This is a week-by-week outline of what you're going to do, broken down by marketing channel. This forms your checklist to make sure everything is happening.

Launch Calendar

Launch Date: *insert final launch date*

Weeks	1	2	3	4	5	6	7	8	9
				Launch Phase 1					
Events	Launch starts			Big Trade Show		How to webinar	How to webinar		
Message	Website is Live!	Website is Live!	Book a run through at the trade show	Book a run through at the trade show	Need help switching over	Need help switching over	Need help switching over	Need help switching over	Need help switching over
Sales Team									
Call centre									
Email									
Press Ads									
Press Releases									

First, create as many columns as there are weeks in your Launch period. Number them. Then add in the predicted dates of those weeks (of course you won't know the actual dates until the Live date is finally confirmed).

Below this, add rows for the following:

- Events
- The overall message each week
- One for each marketing channel you'll be using. You may want to add two rows for some marketing channels — e.g., if the sales team or email marketing is contacting both new and existing customers, it would be worth having one row for each target group.

Then simply (!) fill in the rows.

For the events row, add anything important that might affect the launch: New catalogue goes live, conference, sales person on holiday, etc.

The message might not change from week to week, but it should be acknowledged here as a reminder of what the key message is!

On the row of each marketing channel, note what you'll be doing within that channel each week.

For some channels (like Email), you'll have something different happening at least once a week.

For others (the sales team), it might be the same every week.

And for others (like events), there might just be something in one of the weeks.

This will take a bit of time to create. The first draft often has substantial holes and screams "you'll never hit the objectives with this"! I find that sleeping on it, and revisiting it a few times tends to iron out those kinks.

Once you've got the plan, you'll know exactly what you and the rest of the team need to do and when.

You can download an example and template via: eCommerceMasterPlan.com/freeb2b

A written guide to the plan

It doesn't need to be more than a couple of pages but, if you have several people working on implementing the plan — especially if they're across multiple teams, it is really helpful for making sure everyone understands what is happening and why.

The primary role of this part of the plan is get everyone bought in, so if the written aspect doesn't work for you, maybe it's a video, or a presentation.

The aim is to have something that adds colour to the calendar and tracking dashboard, something you can hand to the rest of the team to explain why you're doing the marketing that's planned.

You can download a template via eCommerceMasterPlan.com/freeb2b.

The target tracking dashboard

Unfortunately, just knowing what marketing you want to do and when and getting the team on board with the written plan isn't enough; you also need to make sure the launch marketing is achieving the objectives.

This is your launch performance tracker. It shows the costs and results (against your objective) of each marketing channel, and is critical in helping you make sure your launch is a success.

As you can see from the image below – it doesn't have to be complicated, but it's essential for making sure you stay focused.

It's going to help you keep on budget. It's going to show you what is and isn't working.

If you're running a phased launch I suggest you create a tracking dashboard for each of your phases, as well as an overall dashboard.

Launch Target Tracking Dashboard				Updated:	end wk 3	
Objective 1:	Get 100 orders placed on the website in first month					
Objective 2:	enter objectives					
Objective 3:	enter objectives					

		Objective 1			Objective 2	
Marketing Method	Orders Placed	Target	Achieved	Actual	Target	Ac
Email	30	50	60%			#
PPC	15	10	150%			#
Untrackable	30	40	75%			#
	75	100	75%	0	0	#

I recommend updating the target tracking dashboard once a week so you always know how well things are going.

With this sort of launch you might not be able to tie the success factors directly to each marketing channel. That's why I recommend you have both the headline launch results AND the performance of each channel outlined.

The temptation with these dashboards is always to include every possible last stat — try not to do that. Keep it to the headline stats that matter; you can dive off and find the others if and when you need them. The essential things to include are:

- Action taken (number of emails sent, number of customers contacted, webinars held)
- Results achieved (email traffic to the new site)

You can download an example and template via: eCommerceMasterPlan.com/freeb2b

Step 6: Execute – Time to Make the Plan Work

Once the Launch Date is finally set, get the dates right in your promotional calendar, and get ready to go!

The most important part of your launch plan is what happens after you finish writing it.

What's going to make your launch as successful as it can possibly be is NOT simply following your promotional calendar to the letter.

What's going to make it super-successful is following the plan for this week, reviewing the results, and tweaking the plan if you need to before you action the next week of activity.

Success is in the optimisation.

"Keep Optimising"

Optimisation is the key to all success in your eCommerce business, in any business to be honest. You should be optimising everything (call centre scripts, website page layouts, products, pricing, customer service standards and, of course, your marketing).

Putting optimisation simply, if something is working well and hitting your targets:

- Do more of it, put more resources behind it.
- Learn why it's doing well and make it even better.

If something isn't doing well and is not hitting your targets:

- Do less of it.
- Consider stopping it altogether.
- Tweak it to make it work for you. Work out which parts of it aren't working and fix them.

It's pretty straight forward: Find the bad, make it better; find the good, keep doing it.

Throughout the Launch (and forever after), you're going to be optimising continuously. Each week when you update the performance dashboard, review the results and decide what needs to be changed.

That might mean running more webinars, sending more emails, cancelling the rest of the SMS sends, or having a chat with the sales team.

To be able to optimise, you need to keep a close eye on performance to see what's working and what isn't.

I suggest you take a top-down approach. Look at the high-level performance of the launch first: Are you on track? Then look at each marketing channel - delve down into the detail where there are issues, or opportunities. This will enable you to look at what you need to, when you need to.

For each marketing channel, there are different things to look at in order to measure success and enable optimisation. For email marketing, you'll want to look at the open rates, click-through rates, and how different segments performed. If you want to understand how to measure and optimise each individual marketing method, you'll read lots more on the key KPIs for each marketing channel in my book "eCommerce Marketing", available now at: eCommerceMasterPlan.com/books

Of course, the ultimate optimisation is if you realise that your objectives were wrong in the first place.

Maybe your launch plan is going to destroy them, and you're on track to beat them by 200%. Then you need to ask the question: Do we want to continue with the full launch and beat the target by 200%? Or do we want to stop when we hit the target? Or do we want to raise the target and see if we can hit 300%? One of those will be the right decision for the business.

Maybe your launch plan, no matter what you do, just isn't working and you're only going to achieve 10% of the target. That suggests there's a fundamental issue somewhere, so it's back to the drawing board. Is the website right? Do the customers want it?

What Happens After Launch?

The end of your launch is the beginning of your success, not the end of it.

You now need to construct your plan — for the website and the marketing — for the next period. If your business works in quarters, then a quarterly plan. If the business works in 6-month stages, a 6-month plan.

The important thing is — you need that plan.

The objectives, the budget, the messages, the marketing methods, the plan, and the execution.

Yes, you can use the 6 steps to plan your launch and to plan the rest of your marketing activity, too. It is the same process.

The only difference is that, once launch has happened, you have some results you can learn from to make your plans even better.

Keep Optimising!

What Next?

Jot down your thoughts.

You've now finished the 4 Stages that should have led you to plan, build, launch, and manage a successful B2B eCommerce store.

Unfortunately, your work is far from over.

You must keep optimising if you're going to stay successful and grow. Optimising the whole business.

So, re-read the Stages and case studies — all have advice that will help you.

The bonus chapter on successful websites will help you make your website work better for your customers.

If you now have the eCommerce bug, you might want to consider selling direct to the consumer. There's a LOT to consider before you do that. So if you're tempted, take a look at the bonus chapter about B2C.

It doesn't all end with this book either. Why not:

- Subscribe to my podcast? The eCommerce MasterPlan Podcast is completely free and filled with inspiration and ideas
  eCommerceMasterPlan.com/podcast

- Read one of my other books. This is my fifth, and they're all about eCommerce
  eCommerceMasterPlan.com/books

- Attend the eCommerce MasterPlan Virtual Summit. It's free and filled with great sessions to help you optimise your business
  eCommerceMasterPlan.com/summit

- Or you could just get in contact for a chat via
  eCommerceMasterPlan.com/contact

16 Case Study: Ramp Tshirts

'Less than 20% of our sales come from people who have zero human interaction pre-purchase'

ramptshirts.com

NEIL COCKER AND his business partner founded Ramp T-shirts in early 2016 and, 12 months in, have a six-figure turnover. They have the world's fastest, smartest custom T-shirt ordering site for teams and events, so getting the website and marketing right is critical to their success.

Yet, more than 4 of every 5 buyers have a human interaction with the Ramp team before they buy.

Ramp doesn't manufacture its product either — they have relationships with T-shirt producers around the world who do the printing and despatching for them. It's all about the order-taking channel — the website.

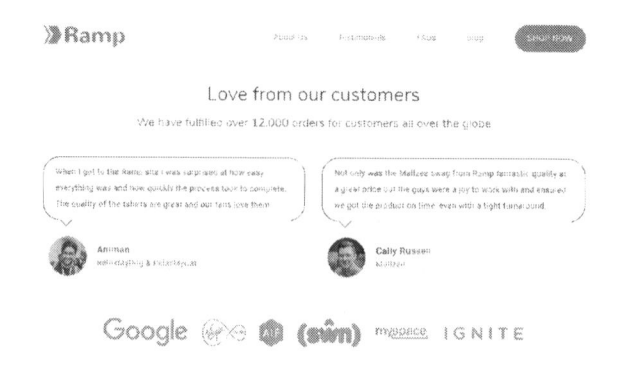

Constant Improvements

The site is high-revenue, low-traffic, so every 1% improvement they can make to the marketing or how the site converts has a big impact on sales and profitability.

As Neil says: "We are all about scale, which is why efficiency is absolutely key to us".

They constantly watch the passage of people through the website (through the funnel — homepage, to product page, to order page) to see how many are progressing at each step.

And they watch actual customer journeys (using Hotjar) to see where people are having problems or spending lots of time.

One of the problems they found was that customers got stuck trying to work out how many of each size they needed. That's essential for placing the order, but complex to get to grips with. So, they now have a calculator, powered by a very clever algorithm, that will predict the sizes the customer needs to order — problem solved.

Online Customer Service

Live chat has been an absolute key to their growth. It enables customers to quickly ask questions and get answers during the buying process. By providing a great customer service experience, it's enabled the Ramp team to build enough trust with their customers that they're willing to place their large orders.

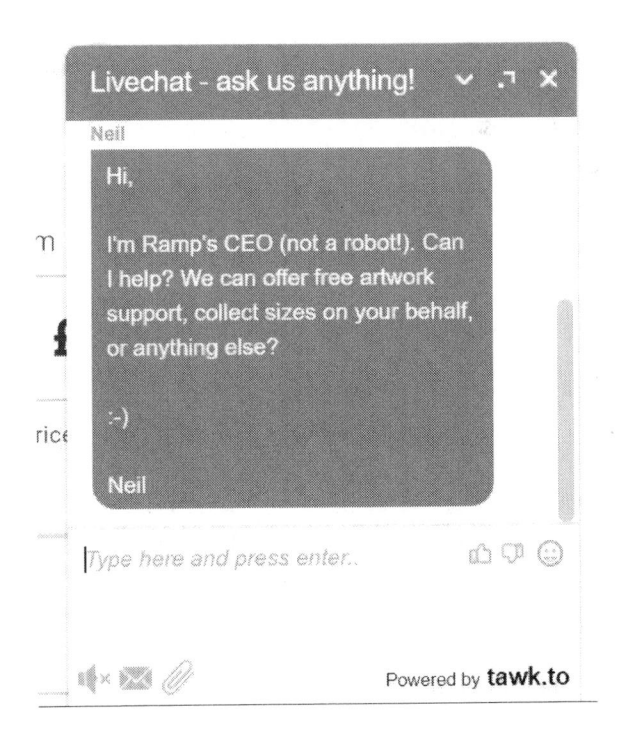

It's also a great source of customer feedback — all those 'stupid' questions people ask (there are of course no stupid questions!). In the early days, people were asking "how much is a t-shirt?" — 'stupid' because all the prices were on the website, and because Ramp doesn't sell single t-shirts, they sell multiple t-shirts to each customer.

From this, they knew they had to make the user experience on the website simpler so people could easily see both the total price, and the price per t-shirt.

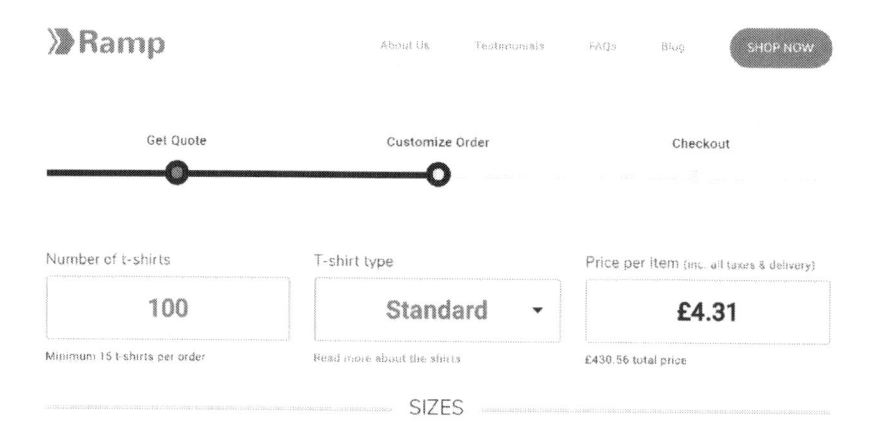

Great Customer Experience Leads to Great Sales

In B2B, you can never ignore the power of referrals as a way to get new customers. For Ramp, it's one of the key growth channels, so it's essential to make sure every customer gets that great experience.

It also leads to repeat orders; if a customer gets a great experience buying T-shirts for this year's event, they'll be back next year to buy again.

Hear more about the Ramp Tshirts story on the eCommerce MasterPlan Podcast episode 123. Listen and get the transcript at: eCommerceMasterPlan.com/freeb2b

17 What Successful Websites Need...
Bonus

Just like you need a launch and marketing plan to get your customers using your website, you also need to put in some effort to make sure your website is doing its job as well as possible.

Just like the marketing will never stop, improving your website is a never-ending task. There's always another stone of optimisation to overturn, and customer behaviour is always adapting too.

The Role of Your Website

Whatever other customer functionality you've built into your website, a good B2B eCommerce website must get the order from the customer.

Marketing → Website → Orders

The most important thing it does is enable the self-service placing of orders, both to give the customer a nice easy, timesaving, convenient experience, AND to stop them using your other channels when they don't need to.

If the website doesn't make it easy for them to place orders, your customers might:

- Regress to their old habits and forget about the website completely, then go back to fax, email, phone call, answerphone, etc.

- Place some orders online, but still place orders via your call centre too.

This completely undermines the whole point of putting the website up in the first place.

AND it means much of the effort you put into launching and marketing the website is wasted.

The key stat for measuring how well your website is doing this is the Conversion Rate.

$$[\text{Traffic}] \times [\text{Average Order Value (AOV)}] \times [\text{Conversion Rate}] = [\text{Sales}]$$

Whilst it is tempting to compare your conversion rate with those of other businesses, or with benchmarks you hear about, I highly recommend you don't. You should only compare your conversion rate within your own business; you are your own benchmark.

The month-to-month comparison of conversion rate for all traffic to the website is a great way to see if things are getting better or worse.

And it's also a great way to compare how successful different traffic-driving methods are (your marketing channels).

If each month you get 1,000 people to your website and your average order value is £500, consider the impact of a better conversation rate:

A POORLY CONVERTING WEBSITE:
Traffic = 1,000
AOV = £200
Conversion Rate = 4.5%

$$[1,000] \times [£200] \times [4.5\%] = [£9,000]$$

IF THE WEBSITE CONVERTS JUST A LITTLE BETTER:
Traffic = 1,000
AOV = £200
Conversion Rate = 5.5%

$$[1,000] \times [£200] \times [5.5\%] = [£11,000]$$

That's a £2,000 sales increase for every 1,000 visitors to the site. It's not difficult to get a B2B website to convert at 5.5%, but many don't. A well put-together website will also help increase your AOV, thus increasing sales even more.

How Do You Increase Your Conversion Rate?

There are lots of ways you can improve your conversion rate for a short time period:

- Mail a catalogue or other direct mail piece to your best customers.
- Send a piece of email marketing.
- Run a massive discount on all products.
- Promote a free P&P weekend.

These are all good marketing ideas, but they aren't improving how well your website does its job. They're just giving the customers a greater incentive to persevere until they've managed to place the order.

So how do you create a permanent improvement in conversion rate? How do you make your website do a better job?

You make it easier for your customers to buy.

Make It Easier for Customers to Buy

This is an endless process. That is all about identifying why customers are failing to buy, and fixing whatever the problem is.

Think of your website like an obstacle course. Your customers are trying to get to the end, but there are lots of obstacles in their way. Things like:

- Logging in
- Postage details
- How fast the page loads
- Being 100% sure that's the item they want to order
- Ordering the right quantity
- Finding the product in the first place
- Finding other information they need
- Knowing when the product will arrive
- Adding the product to the basket

To ensure your website does its job properly, you need to make it as easy as possible for the customer to complete the obstacle course, turning it into a stroll in the park.

That means removing as many barriers to conversion as possible.

A barrier to conversion is anything that stops the customer from buying from you. Most are based on distraction, confusion, or uncertainty. The last two result in a customer getting frustrated, which may lead to them buying from the competition instead of you.

- If a customer is confused, they won't buy.

- If a customer is uncertain that what you are selling is what they want, they won't buy. If they get distracted, they'll forget to buy.

Not every barrier to conversion is within your control. If the phone rings and they have to answer it, which distracts them from placing the order, there's not much you can do about that!

That does still leave plenty that you can work on. Most of these will be fairly unique to your business, customers, and website, but there are some common one-size-fits-all improvements you can make.

The rest of this chapter will take you through some of the general tips and explain how to start identifying the specific problems on your site and how to fix them.

Your eCommerce website is at the centre of your business. If it doesn't work, your business will fail. Invest as much time and money as you can into getting it right, but invest wisely.

Top Tips for Making It Easier to Buy on Your Website

Before you start getting involved in the complexities of conversion rate optimisation (CRO), this is a set of ideas that work in most cases to improve conversion rates.

It's worth working through these before you start a full CRO process.

- **Navigation in the Checkout:** Take a look at Amazon's checkout; once you are in the basket, there's nothing you can do but proceed with your order.

- **Buttons**: Are your buying buttons easy to follow? Do you always put the button to proceed in the same place and in the same colour? Are the words on the buttons clear and do they promote an action? 'Buy now' will work better than 'Buy'.

- **Hidden Postage Costs**: Make sure your customer is aware of postage options early on, as soon as they get to the website. Lots of people will drop out if they get to the checkout and suddenly get hit with a delivery charge they weren't expecting.

- **Delivery Speeds**: Be upfront about these too. When people buy, they want to know when they are going to receive their order.

- **Stock Availability**: Make it clear what is in stock, and, if something is out of stock, when it will be back in.

- **Contact Details**: Don't hide them. Let people know how to call or email you, and explain how fast you'll get back to them if they do. They may well not call, but if they know they can, then that reduces their uncertainty and increases their trust in you. Your address is important, too.

- **Live chat**: A box that pops up on the website and flags the opportunity for customers to ask a question right there and then if they're at all stuck.

- **Product Information**: With the exception of delivery, this is the major cause of confusion and uncertainty.

Include the information the customer needs. Sizes, dimensions, and the right prices are key.

- **Product Photos**: If the dress is available in blue, the customer needs to see the whole dress in blue, not just a swatch of that colour.

- **Promotions**: Make 'em simple. Really simple. If there's anything complex, then keep explaining what the customer needs to do.

Trust[37]

There is one thing you can do to improve conversion across the board, and reduce the impact of customer confusion, uncertainty and distraction — prove that customers can trust you.

If they trust you and like you, they are going to persist a little more to make that purchase; they are less likely to be confused, and they will trust that the areas they are uncertain about will be OK and, if not, they know you will honour a refund. A customer who trusts you is far more likely to remember to come back post-distraction and make the purchase.

Whatever your relationship with your customers, there are a few things you can do on the website to help build that trust:

- Add security logos of the credit cards you accept to the site, and for whichever service you are using to secure your payment area — Sagepay, Verisign, etc.

---

37 This is very closely aligned to social proof, as discussed Chapter 14.

- Have a proper Privacy Policy and Terms and Conditions — and don't hide them. Writing them so they can be read easily is also helpful.

- Fix anything that's broken.

- Have clear and easy-to-find delivery and returns policies.

- Think about adding a guarantee.

- Have an 'About Us' page; show who you are. And include your company history.

- Awards help, too.

- Look at what questions customers regularly ask and write answers to them — FAQs.

- Customer testimonials on non-product pages from homepage to checkout.

- Product reviews — stars, and written reviews on the product pages.

- How many review stars your business has.

Basically, anything that demonstrates how others trust you helps to demonstrate to the person on the website that you can be trusted. This might be press coverage, your size, famous customers — there are so many options.

CRO: The Ongoing Process of Making It Easier to Buy on Your Website

Once you've covered the basics, if you want to improve your conversion rate further, and get your website doing an even better job for you, it's time to start a conversion rate optimisation (CRO) process.

1. Find a barrier
2. Identify a fix
3. Apply the fix
4. Does it work?

CRO is the process of finding the biggest barriers to conversion, working out what should fix them, applying the fix, and seeing if it works.

1. Find a barrier

Finding the barriers starts with looking at the website performance statistics. Where are customers leaving the website? At which point in the buying process are they giving up? What products are most often put in the basket but not bought?

You need to pick one of all the barriers you find to fix first; go for the one that is the biggest problem.

Key tools for this:

- Google Analytics
- Hotjar

2. Identify a fix

Look at the point on your website where the problem is, and see if you can see an obvious solution.

If you can't, then it's time to ask the customers why they are getting stuck at that point.

Key tools for this:

- Deploy a live chat in the problem area.
- Usertesting.com: Set someone up with the challenge and see what happens.
- Any other way to ask the customer about the stumbling block.

3. Apply the fix

Once you've got an idea of how to fix the problem, you need to test it out to see if it is a good idea.

The easiest method is to put the idea live on the site and see if the stats show that you've solved the problem.

The best method is to split test. Have two versions of the page — the original and the new. Show each to 50% of the relevant traffic and see which generates the most sales.

Key tools for such A/B Split testing:

- Optimizely
- Google Optimize

Check to find one that's compatible with your website before buying!

4. Does it work?

An important thing to note here: Whilst we're calling it Conversion Rate Optimisation, really this whole thing is about getting more sales. So, if you find something that gives you a 100% conversion rate, but only generates half the sales of the original page, stick with the original.

If the new version increases your sales, put it live for everyone.

Then repeat the process and move on to the next test.

A few extra CRO tips

Most eCommerce businesses don't get as far as a CRO program like I've outlined above, simply because it's a lot of work. So don't expect to be doing this on day one; do it when the most important thing you need to do is improve your conversion rate.

Those who are actively following a CRO program usually manage just one test per month, so progress is steady but fairly slow.

CRO also incorporates the disciplines of UX and CX:

- **UX** = User Experience
- **CX** = Customer Experience.

They are each slightly different, but both are focused on creating a great user experience to maximise your sales.

If you'd like to know more about CRO, a great starting point would be the three podcasts below:

- **111 Author Interview**: UX Specialist & Author Matt Isherwood, author of "Designing eCommerce Websites — over 50 UX Design Tips and Tricks for Great Online Shops"
- **116 Author Interview**: CRO expert Johann van Tonder joins us to discuss his new book "e-Commerce Website Optimisation".
- **123 Ramp Tshirts's Neil Cocker**: A B2B business with a huge focus on website optimisation.

Listen to those at eCommerceMasterPlan.com/podcast, or you can grab the transcript of each via: eCommerceMasterplan.com/freeb2b

18
Bonus Should You Launch a B2C eCommerce Site?

IF YOU'VE DECIDED to add an eCommerce option for your B2B Customers, you may be thinking 'well, we might as well open it up to consumers too'.

That's another big decision, because it's another totally different business model, and usually requires two websites because the needs of the two consumers are so different. (Obviously this will tweak a bit depending on your products and customers!)

Website Differences

Different product information needs

The B2C Customer will probably only ever buy from you once, so you have to make sure you've given them all the information they need to be able to make that purchase in confidence.

- Lots of product shots.
- Size guides, and spec information.
- Lovely compelling copy about the product to really 'sell' it to them.
- Testimonials and reviews of every product as well as the business overall.
- Delivery information clearly stated – and returns policies.
- And you'll want to be cross-selling other products too.

Some of those are pieces of information that both B2B and B2C buyers need, some are unique to B2C. However, even those that both need, each needs in a different format, layout and priority.

For example, the B2B buyer is usually buying in bulk and repeatedly, so they want it to be easy to buy multiples, to buy several products from one page, with small thumbnails and easy quantity boxes. The B2C buyer is buying one unit at a time, so they need big pictures, full descriptions, and usually the emphasis is on buying one item per order.

Example of a B2C-focused product page

Different pricing needs

Usually, a B2B business will have multiple pricing structures — one for each tier of customer. So the website usually starts with a login so you can identify the business and give them the right prices.

You don't want to start a B2C journey with a login!

You only have one price for all your B2C customers.

Your B2C customers also want to see the final price they pay from the start, full including VAT prices, with likely delivery costs, whilst the B2B customers want to see their unique prices and exVAT the whole way through.

Different checkouts

Often on a B2B eCommerce site, the first thing a customer does is login, so once they get to the checkout all their information is pre-filled.

A B2C customer doesn't want to start on your website by logging in; they want to browse and make their buying decisions. So, you probably know nothing about them until they reach the checkout.

The fewer fields in a checkout the more likely a customer is to check out. A B2C customer doesn't need to give you their VAT information or a purchase order number, but you do need to get their credit card payment, and probably give them an address-lookup service.

Payment methods

A B2C customer wants (usually) to pay by credit card or sometimes PayPal, right there and then. A simple, quick process.

For your B2B customers, you may also be offering the ability to pay via invoice; you don't want to offer this to the B2C customer.

Given all these differences, many of which are quite complex, it may well be simpler to have a separate website for the B2C customer.

Warehouse and Customer Services Differences

Often a B2B business sells products in packs — a pack of 12, a pack of 10, etc. If you open it up to the consumers, you're going to be selling 1 unit, so a pack of 10 will have to be opened. Can your stock system cope with that? Are you happy to sell 1 at retail price, when it may take 12 months to sell the other 9, when you could have sold the pack of 10 at wholesale price tomorrow?

When it comes to shipping the products, B2B is often shipped by the pallet, and definitely in larger boxes than the single items to the B2C buyer.

So you may need different packing materials, and to build relationships with new couriers.

Customer service for B2B customers is usually a different ball game to that for B2C customers. Imagine you're a manufacturer of kids clothing. The B2B customer wants to know when it will arrive, and if you have any offers on hats. The B2C customer wants to know if the Toloula Skirt goes with the Rhinestone Jacket and if (because little Joan has a weirdly large skull) the Blue Fairy T-Shirt neck will cope with being stretched.

The Marketing Differences

With any website, you can't just put it up there and expect the sales to flow. You must do some marketing.

The message and calls to action for the B2B and B2C groups are very different, and it may well be that you find different marketing methods are needed for each.

For B2B, it might be email marketing that alerts them that they haven't yet placed this week's order, or that the new SS collection is ready to pre-order.

For B2C, it might be Facebook Ads to get them in and then emails about key products to get the sale.

That probably means you're going to be doubling everything — marketing plans, budgets, social media accounts, email marketing accounts, online advertising accounts.

The Financial Differences

You're going from orders with an AOV (average order value) in the £100s or £1,000s at a margin you've always been happy with, to orders in the £10s at a much higher margin. But you have to process 100s of them to make the same overall profit as one good B2B order.

Will it be worth it?

The Big One: What About Your B2B Customers?

You risk alienating your core B2B customer base!

If you're a B2B business selling your products to companies who are then selling to the public... how are they going to feel if you start selling to their customer as well? Will they think you're competing?

You're going to become a competitor to your customers — in some form or other.

How to manage that varies from business to business, but a few common approaches are:

- Promise to never undercut them.

- Segment by range, so either there's product that only you will ever sell, or product that you'll never sell.

- Have a stockists page so your B2C eCommerce site links to your B2B Customer sites as well.

- Sell the products they don't want to! Maybe there are replacement parts that your B2B customers don't want the hassle of explaining or stocking? (Read more about this in the Upgrade Bikes case study at the end of Stage 1)

- Launch it under a different brand so they don't realise you're doing it.

Is There a B2C eCommerce Option for You?

Above I've outlined some of the worst-case scenarios for you.

All those differences may not exist in your business; your B2B and B2C customers might be so similar in how they buy that you can serve them through the same site.

Or maybe you have to have two?

You may also find that your best route to maximise B2C margins is to sell on a marketplace (Amazon, eBay, etc,) rather than via a site of your own.

Here's a few real life approaches that I hope will help you decide if you should go B2C…

Homespares runs separate websites for the B2B and B2C customers. Find out how they differ and why they differ in our interview with them.

Party Packs runs one site for everyone and their sales are split equally between B2C and B2B customers. Find out how this works for them in our interview with them.

You can listen to the podcast, or download the transcript of either interview from eCommerceMasterPlan.com/freeb2b

Case studies

Within this book you'll find the following case studies:

- **Upgrade Bikes — Chapter 3**: Going eCommerce to help their B2B Customers sell more.

- **Industrial Ancillaries — Chapter 8:** Making eCommerce a central part of the B2B sales mix.

- **Gloveman — Chapter 12**: Using eCommerce to streamline customer management and improve customer service.

- **Ramp Tshirts — Chapter 16**: An online system, dependent on optimisation and customer services.

You can find many more B2B eCommerce stories in our podcast – find a full list of the various B2B eCommerce businesses Chloë's interviewed on the show right here:

eCommerceMasterPlan.com/B2B-eCommerce-Podcast

Glossary

Whilst there are a lot of eCommerce terms in the book, there's just a few I felt deserved to have easy-to-find explanations.

- **UX, aka User Experience**. The science of improving the users' experience on your website so that you increase your sales.

- **CX, aka Customer Experience**. A step on from user experience. It's about improving every aspect of a customer's experience with your business.

- **AOV, aka Average Order Value**. Pretty self-explanatory. This might be calculated over a set period of time, for a customer segment, or a marketing method. It's a very useful way to compare performance.

- **Direct Despatch.** When you ship products direct to the end consumer on behalf of your B2B customer(s).

- **EDI, aka Electronic Data Interchange.** Any system that enables a B2B customer to automatically feed an order to your system from their system

- **Duplicate Content.** An SEO term. It's when the same content (sentences and paragraphs) appears on multiple websites. The search engines like unique content, so there are fewer rewards for using duplicate content.

- **Broadcasts.** These are the emails you send to your whole list on a regular basis. They are all one-offs and are not part of an automated sequence.

- **CRO, aka Conversion Rate Optimisation.** A catch-all phrase covering all the many ways in which you can improve the conversion rate of your website, usually by changing things on the website itself.

- **CTA, aka Call To Action.** This is the statement in any piece of marketing or on the website that tells the customer what to do — that calls them to action. It can be as simple as "Buy now" on a button.

- **Demographics.** A way to profile people, usually focused on simple data such as age and gender.

- **PPC, aka Pay Per Click.** Any type of online marketing where how much you pay is based on how many clicks you get.

- **SEO, aka Search Engine Optimisation.** Covers the huge range of things you can do to try and make your website more likely to appear in the search engine results (usually Google).

- **Social Proof.** Essentially anything that proves other people like your business.

- **Conversion Rate.** The rate at which traffic to your website converts into orders. It's really useful for tracking how your website performance improves over time, and comparing how good different sources of traffic are — your marketing channels.

About the Author

Author, international speaker, podcast host, and eCommerce advisor.

Chloë Thomas has been working in eCommerce since 2003, always focused on how to increase orders cost effectively through both customer retention, and new customer acquisition.

Over the years, she has worked for and advised businesses large and small, online only and omnichannel, in both the B2B and B2C sectors, and across a wide range of products.

Chloë founded eCommerce MasterPlan in 2012 with the launch of her first book, and it continues to be where she consolidates all her eCommerce and marketing experience to help eCommerce business owners and marketers make the right decisions. Chloë helps them work out what to do next, to optimise their marketing, or be certain the path they're following is the right one for them and their business.

Chloë's advice and guidance is available to all in her books, podcasts, and speaking events.

Her direct help in your business is available in her courses, programs, and mastermind groups, and to a select few businesses in one-to-one advisory sessions and projects.

Power Retail (Australia) named Chloë as one of the top ten eCommerce commentators in the world, and within six months of launch, the podcast was already the top eCommerce podcast in the UK.

Chloë currently lives in rural Cornwall, in the far southwest of the UK, and spends a lot of time sipping peppermint tea on the train to and from London. When she's not thinking about eCommerce and marketing, she makes the most of all that's great about Cornwall — the beer, the food, the beaches, and the rugby.

Praise for Chloë's work:

"Chloë has once again done what she does best and distilled the knowledge of professionals into a MasterPlan guide that a small business owner can not only understand but can implement to grow their business. Everything you need to know is distilled down into a simple framework that's easy to follow and will help accelerate the growth of your business."
Chris Dawson, Editor, Tamebay

"I find Chloë's books and advice invaluable."
Jim McDowell, Marketing Director, Sarah Raven

"[From the project Chloë undertook for us] there were some quick wins... and other areas that we're still working on – all in all the cost will be paid for many times over."
Mike Taylor, Northern Pet Company

"Chloë has a great system for analysing your marketing funnel that helps you figure out where to best focus your marketing efforts."
Dan Adler, Winkbeds.com

Find out more about Chloë at eCommerceMasterPlan.com

Other Books by Chloë Thomas

This is just the latest in Chloë's series of books about eCommerce strategy and marketing.

They are all available as paperback, audiobook, and eBook, and selling in all the usual places.

eCommerce MasterPlan: Your 3 Steps to Successful Online Selling

Explains the important theories behind eCommerce success, and maps out the fastest path to success.

eCommerce Marketing: How to Get Traffic That Buys to Your Website

Really just does what it says — outlining the 9 key marketing methods you should understand to build your business and how to approach them.

eCommerce Delivery: How Your Delivery Strategy Can Increase Your Sales

Takes you through how to use your Delivery Strategy to your advantage, to increase the chances of getting both the first and repeat purchase.

Customer Persuasion: How to Influence Your Customers to Buy More and Why an Ethical Approach Will Always Win

All about growing your business. Identifies the 6 Customer Relationship Levels and how to move customers along to the next one — as that's the key to growing your business.

Find out how to buy at:

eCommerceMasterPlan.com/books

The eCommerce MasterPlan Podcast

The eCommerce MasterPlan Podcast is available totally for free, via iTunes and other podcast apps — or you can listen directly on the website.

You'll find information about all the shows here:

eCommerceMasterPlan.com/podcast

Named in 2017 as one of the 15 Best Podcasts That Ecommerce Entrepreneurs Should Be Listening To by Referral Candy[38], we now have over 100 episodes available.

They are mainly interviews with eCommerce business owners and marketers from businesses of all shapes, sizes, and methods. All have one thing in common — an interesting story to share. Plus, interviews with some selected eCommerce experts, authors, conference takeaways, and the occasional solo show by Chloë.

The aim of every show is to provide you with a dose of inspiration to help grow your business.

If you want to dive straight into just the B2B content, you'll find that here:

eCommerceMasterPlan.com/B2B-eCommerce-Podcast

The 4 most recent reviews from iTunes:

> *Really enjoy this podcast - insightful interviews, wide range of ecommerce business content from marketing to business organisation. I take a lot of inspiration from the entrepreneur stories - recommended for all digital professionals to grow their wider understanding*
> **Adamp29, UK**

---

38   www.referralcandy.com/blog/ecommerce-podcasts/

Essential listening for anyone in or thinking of being in e-commerce. Even if you aren't running an ecommerce business, this has thousands of great tips and nuggets for running your business. The insights offered by both the interviewees and the interviewer and worth their weight in gold. I regularly re-listen to old podcasts. I also recommend Chloe's books which can be applied to business in general not just commerce. Chloe is easy to listen too, the podcasts flow really well and she never shies away from asking the questions that you are dying to ask yourself. She is especially good at making clear where to get all the tools, recommendations and help.
Chrisnic66, UK

I've been in eCommerce for years and finding a podcast which is directed to my issues is absolutely great. Chloe's insight and choice of great guests makes this a great podcast. Thanks Chloe.
SorenHansen, Denmark

Chloe and her guests share inspiring and actionable lessons to help you grow your eCommerce business (without losing your life in the process!). Highly recommend listening and subscribing if you want to improve and grow your eCommerce business!
ErikBison, USA

Made in the USA
Columbia, SC
12 October 2017